Praise for R

I first knew Arianne as a patient, but she very quickly became an inspiration. In *RISE UP,* Arianne Missimer teaches us how to take on life's challenges head on, without retreating or losing our humanity. She shows us that the most important thing is to keep moving, literally. I think of her as equal parts angel and warrior. Knowing her has changed my life and I hope you give her a chance to have that effect on you.

~William P. Levin, M.D.

This important book takes us through a first-hand journey of joy, excitement, trauma, grief, courage, perseverance, and ultimately, happiness. Dr. Arianne Missimer lets us in to the inspirational story of her life, and the events that have led to her current success as a clinician, movement professional, entrepreneur, and athlete. Her story demonstrates how factors such as movement, mindset, and nutrition can quite literally get you through just about any obstacle -- and she has certainly faced her share of obstacles. Upon finishing this book, you can't help but feel inspired to *RISE UP* and take control of your life.

~Dr. Chris Leib, DPT

This book is a true testament to how powerful your gift of movement is. You'll be taken on an incredible journey through the highs and lows of life, all of which made an inspiring story about an amazing woman. I highly recommend this book to anyone who needs inspiration to keep pushing through especially during the tough times, but more importantly make sure you have fun while doing it!

~Kevin Cantwell

I do NOT read books but this book kept my interest. I couldn't put it down! It was so real and drew me in. It's like I was right there experiencing the events right along with her from beginning to end. Great book!!

~ Amy Nemcic

Dr. Missimer's incredible journey would not have been possible without her courage, grit, resilience and determination! Rise Up gives a first-hand look at how to meet all of life's challenges head on in a positive way. As you read each chapter you can almost feel her passion for life and her desire to always keep learning. Dr. Missimer's joy is contagious and you will find yourself smiling along with her as she recounts learning to dance and feeling that lump in your throat as she shares some of her darker days. Rise Up leaves you feeling that you can tackle any obstacle in your path using Dr. Missimer's mantra "Challenge Accepted!" A great read!
~ Pat Dunn

RISE UP is Dr. Arianne Missimer's heroic journey through trauma, loss, grief, and cancer. The book gives insight into how she was able to harness the hardship into triumph, never allowing it to break her spirit and taking her all the way to American Ninja Warrior. This is a truly inspirational story and I would recommend to anyone going through their own struggles who wants to find strength within themselves to overcome life's many hard challenges.

~ Karen Catalfamo

Arianne Missimer's unfolding story on the pages of *RISE UP* allows the reader the opportunity to follow along on her journey of ups and downs and see how the power of movement, nutrition, and a healthy mind-set can lead to self-healing. This book is for anyone who has experienced obstacles, challenges, or difficulties and will inspire them to RISE UP and push thorough!

~ Wendy Farrell

Rise Up

Journey of Healing Through
MINDSET • NUTRITION • MOVEMENT

DR. ARIANNE MISSIMER

The Happy
Self-Publisher
publish.smile.repeat

www.happyselfpublisher.com

For you…. who has faced their own challenges in life, may you be empowered and inspired to appreciate your health and the gift of movement, be the best version of yourself, and have the strength to *RISE UP*.

Contents

Foreword

I was awkwardly waiting in the gym vestibule, wearing khakis and a scratchy polo on my first day as an athletic trainer covering hours at Kinetic, a physical therapy (PT) clinic. My nerves felt like they were consuming me. Yet, as soon as this green-eyed, blonde-haired, bubbly woman walked in, I couldn't help but feed off her positive energy.

My first day turned out to be very memorable, and all due to that very special person named Arianne Missimer.

We shook hands and, before I could even introduce myself, I felt like we had known each other for years. Little did I know exactly how amazing she was right away, but I would quickly find out. I'll never forget how, at the end of that first shift, she made a point to look me in the eye and say, "Thank you so much, Becky, for everything you did today." Just the way she said it made me feel important, as if I was truly contributing to the company.

She made me feel like I was part of the Kinetic team right away: someone who made an impact on every patient who walked through the door. Arianne simply has this special way about her that makes you feel like you genuinely matter.

I observed a PT before, which I never really thought was anything special. That's why I initially chose to stick with athletic training as my job of choice. A career path leading me toward PT was not part of my plan.

Yet the longer I worked with Arianne, the more I had a mindset shift. After only a few months of interacting, we had bonded and she claimed me as her sidekick. I worked with all her patients, and I soaked in every piece of education she gave me on movement. Watching Arianne work helped me realize that what she did and how she did it was actually something I could see myself doing, too.

She was always treating the whole body and finding ways to incorporate functional movement into every exercise, all while dancing and laughing through the day. She had passion and so much love for movement, which was evident whenever you talked to her patients or coworkers.

This woman lived out her advice. She worked as a PT, owned her own business, and exercised for fun. Her love of movement very quickly rubbed off on me; and before I knew it, my true passion was much more than mere athletic training. So, when I asked her for professional advice about my next career path and she, without hesitation, told me PT was the right path, I listened.

Before that point, I'd had advisors, family, and even my husband tell me to do PT. Every time, I would laugh and say, "Never will I ever be a PT." But when Arianne said it, I realized that if such a talented healthcare professional saw my potential in this regard, how could I say no to a career she knew I could excel in?

She helped me realize I did want to be a PT so I could inspire people to move with intention and love every aspect of the gifts they were given.

During my subsequent schooling, my mom was diagnosed with cancer and sadly passed away. Yet I decided to push through my courses anyway and rise up just as Arianne would any time she was faced with a challenge. Her story truly inspired me to be the best version of myself and to see a challenge as an opportunity to grow.

Her story is something special and well worth sharing. I've tried telling my friends so many times about how amazing she is and how lucky I am to work with her. Though, I can never get her story quite right. Who could when telling about a woman who has accomplished so much and inspired so many?

Fortunately, Arianne has finally put that story in writing for all of us to see how she's become the woman she is today. She describes her journey through her life accomplishments. While those accomplishments are amazing, the journey itself has always been her favorite part, not so much the destination.

With each chapter she tells, you can see the challenges she had to face — but you will also see how she found a way to rise up and become stronger from each one. You will laugh with her during her silly moments and cry with her during her most trying times. All the while, you will feel the genuine love that always surrounds her through family, friends, patients, and coworkers.

Although, mostly through her.

I am truly blessed to be introducing such an amazing woman's story. She was inspired to write a book about how mindset, nutrition, and movement helped her rise up, and I hope her journey inspires you as well, just as it has inspired me to move, love, laugh, and cry… but, more importantly, to never back down when faced with a challenge. Just as Arianne did, rise up!

As she's proven time and time again, it's worth the effort.

Dr. Rebecca Quintangeli, PT, LAT, ATC

1

A Dream Come True

*I*t was December 3, 2018, and John and I were sitting at a table with First Resource Bank. I was in my fitness clothes, as usual – yoga pants, a tank top, and a fitness jacket with my minimalist barefoot shoes. John was dressed professionally, as usual – dress shirt and khakis with his brown hair, green eyes, and adorable dimples. Meanwhile, Frank Englund, our excellent realtor, was to our right; and Fran, our mortgage broker, to our left.

Then there was Charles Barr, the current owner of the 5,000 square-foot building we were in the process of purchasing. He sat across the table, smiling from ear to ear as John and I signed document after document with signature after signature. Honestly, it seemed like it would never end.

Perhaps that was because I felt like we were signing our lives away.

Maybe we were?

My heart was beating faster, and my breath was a bit more shallow than usual as I looked at John. That's when I noticed he had a bit of a deer-in-the-headlights look too. So, at least it wasn't just me.

Yet after an hour of signing documents and reviewing the details, there we were... the new proud owners of 101 Manor Avenue, Downingtown, Pennsylvania – which meant that, a moment later, they weren't just handing me any set of keys. They were handing me the keys to my dream practice, The Movement Paradigm Integrative Health Center.

This was an enormous deal. It felt unreal for so many reasons, including how I'd felt like I was on my deathbed three years ago to that very day. Although, there I was now, with my supportive and loving husband living out my dream. How had so much happened in such a small span of time?

I remember envisioning my own multidisciplinary practice: a place where I could truly treat the whole person – not just their most obvious physical symptoms, but the movements and mentalities behind those issues. The body is so complex, I thought. How could you just simply look at one aspect of health and consider it a cure-all?

At this place of mine, there would be nutrition, movement, physical therapy, massage, psychology, yoga, and more. That's how I pictured it. I knew that's what people deserved: a place where they could come to heal their bodies, improve their health, move well and often, and live with vitality.

I had already started my first business three years before that dream really began to form. At 22 years old, CORE Fitness Studio became my business baby, which I poured so much time and energy into every day. My team and I always strove to be so much more than personal trainers. I never wanted to be just another fitness center. I really wanted us to make a difference in our clients' lives: to teach people how to truly take care of their bodies emotionally, mentally, and physically.

Now here I was, taking that dream to its next level – something bigger and more effective than ever.

"John, is this really happening?" I think I needed to hear him say it if I was going to accept such an amazing accomplishment. I threw my arms around his six-foot-three frame and hugged him like I've never hugged him before. I was grinning ear to ear in excitement and felt this immense sense of gratitude filling my body. "I can't believe it! Thank you! Thank you! Thank you!"

"For what?" he asked with his charming smile.

"For believing in me. For supporting me. For helping me make this happen." I ran out of exact details at that point, too caught up in the moment. "For everything!"

There really was a lot to thank him for, too. Leaving a great job with stability, benefits, and insurance is always a risk. The way both of us saw it, taking that risk to do what you were meant to do – what you truly love and believe in – to live out your purpose is vitally important. That's a mantra I've long since held, and John was exceptional in supporting me in that, as he'd once again proven.

I remember when I approached Corina Schad, owner of Presence in Mind and Body, the year before. I wanted to see if she'd like to be part of the Movement Paradigm Integrative Health Center, already well aware that she is one of the most lovely people, from Germany, I might add.

We first met when she took one of my barefoot courses, where we found an instant connection. We both were in love with and downright fascinated by the complexities of the human body, and we had great conversations as a result. Corina is a bodyworker, but so much more than that. She helps individuals release emotions that are stored in their physical bodies, which can be such a powerful experience.

I told her we'd have to connect after the course, and we did. I went to see her. She came to see me. We even began referring clients to each other, trusting each other's expertise and genuine care for our clients.

After getting her on board with my newest idea, I hunted down Joe Chaitkin, a truly great guy. That's what everyone says about him. That's what I say about him, too, adding in how he's also an excellent personal trainer and coach, who owns Align Fitness.

We were initially connected through mutual clients when I was working as a physical therapist at Kinetic Physical Therapy (while still owning and operating CORE Fitness), and Joe was working a few jobs himself. We'd laugh about our busy schedules for the most part, occasionally lending an ear when we were really running around like chickens with our heads cut off and unsure how to handle the stress.

I trusted him every bit as much as Corina, recommending him whenever I could as well. For instance, I had this grand idea a few years back: The Movement Paradigm Summit. It would bring together like-minded experts in the fields of mindset, nutrition, and movement. We'd invite the community and offer them an opportunity to explore new movement disciplines and be exposed to different philosophies on living their best lives.

That did, admittedly, beg a question: How on Earth would I pull this massive project together? To solve that problem, I pitched it to Darren, my then-boss at Kinetic Physical Therapy, and he loved the idea. After helping me work out some logistics, he was totally on board, as he was with most of my lofty ideas.

Then, I pitched my plan to the board at West Chester University. Because, why not? I thought that would be a great location to hold a summit, and I managed to make them see my vision as well, another obstacle down.

It was time to invite the speakers. In which case, I immediately thought of Corina and Joe.

They're exactly the caliber of professionals I wanted to represent the first Movement Paradigm Summit. Better yet, when I asked them, they couldn't have been more excited and honored, not to mention willing.

My great friend Mike Panulla, a karate and QiGong expert and owner of Magnus Karate, also agreed to be a part of it. Somnath, one of the owners of Dragon Gym, who I admire so much, was excited to teach Taekwondo. Even my extremely talented ballroom dance teachers,

Valentine Hodgman and Anna Akarman from the Blue Ballroom, said they would teach some swing dance moves to everyone.

There was also Dr. Chris Leib, one of my friends, mentors, and physical therapy extraordinaire; Andrea Littlewood, also a friend and gifted Pilates teacher; Keli Laverty, a dance movement therapist and licensed professional counselor; and Angie Foster, a dear friend, amazing human, and clowning teacher. They were some of my top recruits, though I enlisted many others, including specialists in tai chi, yoga, nutrition, and more. It kept evolving until I even had three departments of students volunteering: athletic training, exercise, and nutrition. Everyone seemed to want to be a part of it!

I was so excited for the big day! I mean, I'll admit that life's possibilities usually get me excited, but this was phenomenal! I had worked so hard for this to come to fruition. In the end, 125 people registered, which was an impressive number: proof that other people saw the same need that I did.

When I walked in that day, there were so many things to do. I was even more grateful than ever for those individuals who'd agreed to be my volunteers. The time flew by anyway, with one thing to do after another until everything was set up, everyone was seated, and it was go-time. I had the mic in my hand as I took the stage, looking around at these 125 people hungry for this knowledge and experience my expert panel was going to deliver.

Despite the whirlwind of activities, I somehow managed to pause a few times over the course of the day to soak it all in. Mindset. Nutrition. Movement.

My vision.

It was a gamechanger. After that day, everything truly was different – in large part because I knew I could offer so much more. Not only did I know I wanted to treat the whole person; now I realized that many people wanted that, too. It was all becoming more clear to me, though that did raise one important question as a result.

How could I combine all these things? How could I treat my patients and clients with this philosophy – a patient-centered, whole-person approach?

That was when I knew I had to fulfill my dream. I might not have had it all figured out in that moment. But I spent a lot of time the rest of that year reflecting on the task at hand and trying to figure out my direction.

It wasn't until November that I made significant progress, I'll admit. It didn't come to me in one of the most pleasant ways, unfortunately or fortunately, since one of the physical therapists I was supervising at Kinetic decided to resign. I didn't pry too much. That was definitely not the first time someone had stepped down, and I was sure it wouldn't be the last, either.

It would mean I had to go "under."

By that, I mean that I had to continue with my caseload, plus treat the majority of hers. This would have been close to 90 visits per week, in addition to my responsibilities as a clinic director, including marketing and management necessities. On top of that, I was dealing with so many health issues at the time.

I didn't have the energy.

The motivation.

The desire.

I realized I just couldn't do it this time. Not mentally. Not physically. Not emotionally. Part of me felt weak for admitting that to myself – guilty, too. I had done it many times before, after all.

What was different now?

After some thought, I realized that I was different. I knew what I wanted now. I didn't know how I was going to get there, but I was clear nonetheless. It was time; time for me to spread my wings, no matter how crazy or sudden or cliché that sounded.

That realization only helped so much, especially when I was already super-stressed. New stressors filled my mind, like: *They've done so much for me. How could I leave?* And: *Am I going to make it? Will I get enough patients on my own?*

I went home that night and I told my husband, "Babe, I think I'm going to leave Kinetic."

John gazed right back at me, probably more calmly than I was at him. "Do it. We'll make it work."

Just like that, the planning began as we discussed where I would go and how I could keep seeing patients. We threw around a lot of ideas that evening before I made my next most important call. By the time I did, I was feeling a lot more confident.

"Mom," I said into the phone. "I'm going to leave Kinetic."

Always worried at first, her initial response was, "Is everything okay?"

"Yes," I assured her. "I'm going to live out my dream. I'm not sure how yet, but I'm doing it."

As I said those words out loud, the confidence really started to kick in full-gear. I knew I was making the right decision. This was it! It was go-time.

I had been through so much: things that nobody should ever have to face. I had overcome them anyway – somehow. Yet everything that had come before – the bad and the good alike – I now saw had pointed me to this moment. This decision.

When I had done my TEDx talk on overcoming challenges through mindset, nutrition, and movement, *Challenge Accepted*, the year before, I remember how it led me to reflect on my journey and how that contemplation had been so incredibly healing. Perhaps this was part of my healing, too?

I knew when I was 22, after a life-altering event, that I was put here on Earth to change lives. It left me feeling more driven than ever to create a practice.

To create a brand.

To create a community.

To share with others the power of mindset, nutrition, and movement.

To build something bigger than myself.

To shine a light in the world.

So yes. This right here? This right now? It was time. My time to shine a light to people who were suffering from weights they didn't even necessarily understand.

After considering my options, I reached out to Mark Falcone, the owner of iCORE Fitness, a local ninja gym. A good friend, he agreed to let me rent space at his business, which made for the perfect launch pad to get my own off the ground.

My goal was to average 20 visits a week. Let me tell you that I hustled to get each and every one. I did my best to be very present on social media, and I hosted workshops and community events. As I did, former patients and clients reached out to me, some even from CORE Fitness.

It was happening, slowly but surely, and I was loving every single bit of it. I loved seeing my patients for a whole hour and having the opportunity to listen attentively as if there was no one else in the world. I loved being able to give individualized advice as a result.

Every patient or client that sought me out seemed to have been dealing with chronic health issues. A 53-year-old woman who was dealing with chronic low back pain and headaches came to see me. She had been to multiple therapists and doctors. She also had imaging done to show that she had a herniated disk. Of course, I took the opportunity to educate her that her image did not correlate with her pain, as it doesn't in most cases. As she explained her symptoms during her first appointment, she began crying because she felt like she was losing hope that she'd ever feel good again. I listened to every word she had said. She continued to cry and I reached out to give her a big hug, with her consent.

"Thank you. Thank you so much," she said.

After she told me what had been going on for years, in addition to her history of poor sleep habits, chronic gut issues, two c-sections, and chronic stress, I began my evaluation. I found that her feet, her foundation, were not supporting her or her center of stability in her core. Additionally, the scar tissue from her c-sections was affecting her core function. Scars are a normal part of healing; however, can impact the functionality of surrounding and/or distant muscles and organs. A c-section scar, for example, can adhere to the abdominal wall, pelvic floor and surrounding core muscles, and the small intestine, among other organs, preventing the diaphragm, our main muscle of respiration, from descending properly. Even her pelvic floor I found to be a bit overactive.

Breathing is one of the most important aspects of my assessment because it can tell me so much about a person's overall health. For this lovely woman, her breathing pattern was less than optimal. She was not able to take a diaphragmatic breath, where the abdomen expands 360 degrees on the inhale and the abdomen contracts on the exhale. As soon as she took a deep breath, her neck and shoulders rose and her belly button was sucked in towards her spine. These findings alone showed me why she was having back pain and headaches. Of course, I also watched her move, walk, stabilize against resistance, and performed special testing to rule in or out any specific diagnoses.

As our evaluation was nearing the end, I took the time to explain everything in great detail. I explained which movement compensations were contributing to her pain, but I also provided her with some recommendations to begin to address some of the lifestyle factors that were also adding to her chronic pain: sleep, hormones, stress, and inflammation. I went on to give her some vagus nerve stimulation exercises to help create a relaxation response in her body and followed that with some breathwork.

"This will not only help decrease pain, but will also help your core to sequence more efficiently," I explained.

As the weeks went on, I introduced scar massage, pelvic floor relaxation techniques, and began developing a solid movement plan for her to begin lifting weights again. She started slowly changing her sleep habits and began meditating as part of her nightly ritual. She even went on the elimination diet to decrease inflammation in her body and identify food triggers that were contributing to her emotional, mental, and physical issues.

Then one day, at one of her appointments a few months later, I watched her perform a 60-pound deadlift. The lady that cried to me several months ago, who was ready to give up, was now strong, vibrant, and most importantly, happy.

This was me. This was exactly what I was meant to do – even if I fully recognized that the "where" part of the equation wasn't quite there. It was just that I had to first establish that I really could do what I was setting out to do.

Once that was a proven fact, my wonderful husband and I began the search for an official place of operations. We looked all over Downingtown, Pennsylvania; West Chester; and even Coatesville. It was a difficult search, considering how what we were looking for wasn't just any space. It had to be somewhere that would really facilitate healing, which is a pretty tall order.

Our realtors finally found what seemed like the perfect place. It was like a sanctuary, located next to a stream with beautiful woods around it: the integrative health "retreat" I was looking for, through and through.

Unfortunately, after months of business planning and applying for a Small Business Association (SBA) loan, we realized there were environmental issues, as well as some other significant problem spots, that meant my supposed "perfect place" wasn't quite so wonderful after all.

I remember being so disheartened because I couldn't seem to find anything that seemed remotely close to the peace, beauty, and serenity it offered. My vision of the center was becoming so much more clear, but that meant the options were growing so much more slim. We tried expanding our searches too, looking at condominiums to stand-alones to strip malls, yet nothing fit.

Then, we found Frank, a realtor who was referred me by one of my patients. He met John and me at his first pick for us: the Exton Commons, which were condominiums and at the other end of the extreme from our first love. After debating for hours, we decided to keep looking, feeling the weight of yet another dead end – at least that's certainly how I felt.

Then John and I drove past 101 Manor Avenue, which was a beautiful stone and wood building, our favorite combination, with a u-shaped driveway surrounded by a gorgeous stone wall and a stunning beech tree out front. Both of us thought it looked awesome, but I had to point out how it was obviously out of our price range.

"Not so fast," he said.

So, we arranged to look at it after all.

I remember walking in and thinking immediately that I wasn't too sure about it. It was like a maze, with walls and tiny exam rooms everywhere you could imagine. Every time I turned a corner, I seemed to lose my way. The building clearly hadn't been updated since the 1970s with its old paint, worn brown carpet, and faded drop ceilings. Far from its engaging outer appearance, I just did not see the potential. It was really hard to.

John saw it, though. He always saw the possibilities, urging me to consider them when I would otherwise turn away. I listened to him and so, when we got home that night, we put our heads together on how to make it work. What if we made Corina and Joe tenants, and maybe others too? Then, John put together a blueprint showing all the walls we could knock down to open the space.

I had no idea how to make it work on my own, but I followed his lead and kept considering the possibilities. Until, after days of contemplating and trying to find potential tenants, we decided to move forward.

Moreover, I decided to open on January 1, 2019, just one month after our closing date. Of course, that meant we had a lot of renovating to do in a very short span of time. John and I spent evenings after work and full weekends knocking down walls, painting, laying floors, and such. John, being the expert developer that he is, did all the electrical and plumbing work, too.

Really, my husband knew how to do it all. As for me, let's just say I learned a lot—flooring, demolition, painting, and using a saw just to name a few. Better yet, he didn't kill me for not having his level of expertise. Nor did I kill myself – so a win-win-win all around!

When everything was said and done and the new year came around, the place looked absolutely beautiful. There were wood floors, cedar walls, and stone throughout. The beautiful floor-to-ceiling windows shed natural light and warmth to the place. Simply put, it was every bit as engaging and inspiring and yet restful as I'd envisioned.

It was perfect!

Staring at the center around me, I had to smile. This was the dream place. Right in the heart of Downingtown, Pennsylvania, this was the place where I was going to fulfill my purpose. This was where I would make a difference.

This was the place where I would really *rise up* – and show others that they could, too.

2

Where It All Began

When you look back on your childhood, it's always interesting what you remember. Then, of course, there are the things your parents tell you.

My mom still says to this day that I was a pistol. As a very little girl, I always wondered… what does that mean? It might not have been until much later when I was watching some videos of myself when I was six, that I got the picture. I was cheerleading at St. Catherine of Sienna, my grade school – the youngest member on the squad with this oversized t-shirt on, a short pixie haircut, and a grin from ear to ear.

You would have thought I was in charge, or at least that I thought I should have been. I not only knew every move, I did each one with authority.

I was a "pistol" alright.

As my parents would always say, I loved everything I got involved in, particularly if it involved movement or sports. Gymnastics was probably my favorite, though. I went to First State Gymnastics Center when I was six and loved every second and detail of it, including my black-and-white striped leotard.

Whenever I would get the chance, I'd show my moves off to anyone who would watch. Of course, that was only the people that loved me most: Mom, Dad, my brother Davey – when he wasn't irritated with my antics – Grams and Pop-Pop, and my Aunt Dot. They always had a huge smile for me: pure joy that nothing could top. Sometimes, my dad would even do headstands with me in the living room.

After that, I moved on to swimming at Arundel Pool. I loved being on the swim team, but even more so because Grams would take me. Next up, in grade school, I was a three-sport athlete: volleyball, softball, and my all-time favorite, basketball.

Boy, did I love basketball? Though, I worked just as hard at excelling at volleyball. As captain of both teams, I always maintained confidence, positivity, and, most importantly, camaraderie with my teammates.

No matter what I got myself into, my mom and dad were always there supporting me and encouraging me. My dad was a quarterback on his high school football team, who then played quarterback at Oklahoma State University. He was an avid sports fan, so I think I got my love of movement from him. He came to every game and always rooted me on from the stands. In fact, he would tell me what to do before and after the game, too.

"You gotta shoot, Oopie," he would say. "You gotta drive. That's the way to get points. Drive in and get fouled."

Oopie was what he called me. No rhyme or reason for it, as far as I know. "Oopie" just stuck. I always knew I was loved whenever he used it.

Then again, I always knew I was loved no matter what.

As soon as Dad knew I was serious about basketball, he bought me a net for the house so I could practice my foul shots; and practice I did. I wanted to make him proud for sure, but I also wanted to improve my game for myself and my teammates. High school starting lineup, here I come, I told myself.

As for Mom, she cheered me on simply because she loved me. She would do anything she could to make sure my brother and I were healthy and happy.

Mom was always the rock of the family. I remember, even as a child, just how deeply she loved us no matter how by-the-books she was. To the core, she is a rule follower.

Personally, I always liked to bend the rules just a little. I wonder now if that was just to keep her on her toes. Either way, I know I got it that from Dad; he liked to bend the rules, having fun whenever he could, like he was just a big kid.

Despite that little rebellion, she would always hug me and say, "I love you, Rans," her personal nickname for me. I could never figure that one out either, but one thing I did know: There wasn't anyone else in the world who could love me more than she did.

She showed that in so many ways, including through writing. Whether it was a thank-you note, a good-luck note, or an "I'm proud of you" note, she always had a way with words. My mom is truly one of the most special souls walking this Earth.

I feel extremely blessed that my innate compassion, empathy, and work ethic come from my mom and that my love of travel, free spirit, and love of sports comes from my dad. They gave me a truly terrific combination to work with.

Then there was Davey, my big brother. My idol. My reality check.

As any little sister can and will do, I annoyed him regularly, never quite getting why he would roll his eyes so much at me. Considering how my big green eyes were always staring at him in admiration, he coined the name "bug eyes" as his own personal nickname for me. How could I forget that he called me "fat girl," too? Sometimes he would even put them together – "fat girl bug eyes."

Between that, Oopie, and Rans, I might have been at risk of forgetting my real name. Which, I suppose wouldn't have been so bad, since no one ever got it right anyway.

Despite the less-than-flattering designations, I thought Davey was the coolest ever. I actually wanted to be like him, which looking back, may have been what annoyed him so much. There were, no doubt, a few other things that could have done the trick as well.

Looking back on my childhood, I think I could have been a kid forever. In fact, there's part of me that still believes in the magic of Christmas. As in Santa Claus. It's true.

As most young children probably do, I truly believed in Santa Claus. Though, unlike most of them, it wasn't until I was 12 years old that I was (somewhat) dissuaded of the notion. Not just Santa either. The Easter Bunny, too. The evidence was too overwhelming for me to conclude anything else.

Exhibit A: After Santa Claus came down the chimney on Christmas Eve, he always had a few sips of milk and ate some cookies. He even left the crumbs to show it. I knew exactly what the Easter Bunny looked like as he hopped down the street holding lots of baskets for all the kids on our street, too.

Incidentally, while I knew Santa Claus had his warehouse of toys at the North Pole and could carry all the gifts on his sleigh, I never did figure out where the Easter Bunny restocked.

As my mom tells the story, it was Davey who finally brought my wholehearted illusions to an end when he had a talk with Mom. "You have to tell Arianne. She's embarrassing herself."

True enough, I really had already done a pretty good job of that. My friends, for some strange reason, had stopped believing in Santa Claus and the Easter Bunny early on. I do remember one particular afternoon at the school lunch table at St. Catherine of Sienna, surrounded by my friends and classmates, when I defended Santa Claus – one of the many times I came to his defense, I might add.

My argument that time: "There is no way our parents could afford all those presents!"

My imagination was always running wild. I guess that was part of the problem. For instance, I dreamt of having my own horse, envisioning riding on a chestnut beauty in the sunset with the wind blowing through my hair. A bit obsessed, I thought I could eventually win my dad over by asking him almost every single day – even though the answer was always no.

So, I wrote a book called *A Girl's Best Friend*, where I had my own horse, Blazing Star. She was a beautiful chestnut, just like I always imagined, with a single white marking between her eyes – a dream come true.

I wrote about all the amazing adventures we would go on together and had my mom teach me how to use the typewriter to type it out. Then, since I always loved to draw as a kid, taking sketching and painting lessons, and drawing every room in our house, I drew accompanying pictures of Blazing Star. Although very challenging, the results were an excellent accomplishment I was very proud of.

Apparently, Dad was impressed with all my efforts, too. Because he caved. Finally. I must have asked hundreds of times, and it was always a no. But one Tuesday evening, after he had a few drinks, I asked just one more time. He said yes!

"Dad, really!? Really? I can get a horse?" I was over the moon. "Where can we put it?"

"We can put it in the backyard," he told me.

I could barely believe the words. But he had said them. Blazing Star was going to be mine! She was going to jump out from my book – right into my backyard.

Hearing the garage door open, I realized that Mom was home. As she walked in the door, dressed to the nines as always, I screamed in continuing euphoria, "Mom, Dad's getting me a horse!"

I should have known. I really should have. I was, after all, asking Dad for a reason. So, as it turned out, Blazing Star was meant to stay on the pages for a while longer. I didn't completely give up on the idea, mind you, but I guess I did give Dad a rest on the subject.

Looking back, that's a fond memory, even if it did feel crushing at the time. There were much more serious hardships that life sent my and my family's way. Although I can't recall all the details, I do remember when my brother was diagnosed with cancer at 11 years old. It was kind of a blur, though I was oh-so aware that Mom's heart was breaking that whole entire time, no matter how stoic she tried to be.

My dad may have had an even harder time with the situation, since he ended up turning to what he knew out of it – alcohol.

As for me, I wasn't really sure what "cancer" was or why Davey was so sick that I couldn't be with him – or my parents, for that matter. Mom and Dad both thought it would be best if I stayed with Grams and Pop-Pop since they had to stay at Johns Hopkins Hospital in Baltimore, Maryland.

It was a very long journey before he got better, and I prayed for him whenever I could. My teachers at the time were so supportive, and they prayed for him with me, encouraging the rest of the class to do the same. I made him get-well cards, too. I think some part of my young self recognized that these weren't supposed to be "get well" wishes when you have a cold or an inconvenient surgery. They were "get well" so he could live his life again.

They kept saying I was too young to see Davey, which is why I didn't get to go. When they did decide I could visit, I was so excited to see my big brother – my idol!

Some details about that day are still so vivid, these several decades later – like how the hospital felt so cold and how there were lots of white walls everywhere. The nurses and doctors were bustling through the hospital as if someone was chasing them. I noticed that too, and how they seemed nice enough, despite their hurry. Some even gave me a quick smile on their way past.

I also recall waiting patiently outside the elevator with Mom, and how Davey didn't come down alone. One of those busy nurses was in teal scrubs and a hat, and she was pushing him in a wheelchair.

He looked so different to me without any hair, dressed in a hospital gown and socks. He didn't have the same smile that he usually did when he saw me, even though I annoyed him most of the time.

Even so, I couldn't wait to hug him. So, it was quite a disappointment when I found out I wasn't allowed. Worse yet, it seemed like the second that I saw him, they were taking him away again. He was too sick to stay, I was told. All of a sudden, I got it. That's what made everything so real for me.

Davey didn't even look like the brother I knew. The brother who called me "Bug Eyes." The brother who rolled his own eyes at me all the time. The brother who was strong and protective. The brother who I looked up to every day. The brother who I loved so much and the one who I knew loved me too. Even though I aggravated him more than anyone else could, I just knew how much I ultimately meant to him.

That brother of mine was really, really sick.

That weight was a big one for my little self, and my Grams and Pop-Pop made a valiant effort to alleviate what they could. I did love every second of staying with them, I have to admit. They were so kind-hearted. So was my treasured aunt, Dot. They were so good to me.

Although Aunt Dot wasn't my biological aunt, she was one special lady and I loved her so much. She lived with my grandparents, so at least for that time, that meant she lived with me, too. She would do anything for me, just like Grams. Later on, when she did finally get a place of her own, I remember staying at her house on more than one New Year's Eve while my parents went out celebrating. It was so exciting for me.

The best part was that she let me stay up every year until the ball dropped. The only problem was that, right at 12 o'clock, I always wanted to call Mom and Dad to wish them a Happy New Year. As such, I missed the big moment on TV every single year.

As for Grams specifically, I've already said I adored her; and I really, really did. I remember she would let me have mint chocolate-chip ice cream with pretzel crumbles in her bed while I watched my preferred cartoons, like *Dennis the Menace*.

She always spoiled me with love and goodies, and I'll never forget when we would take the bus into town. She never drove, so we got to experience public transportation, which I loved! I had a real baby stroller for my twins – Eric and Erica – and Candy, my "favorite" daughter, all of which I would take with me. They all looked like real babies because I really didn't like any dolls that didn't.

I did have a family of seven at the time, but Grams thought I should only bring three.

We'd get on the bus, fold the stroller up, hold the babies, and wait to arrive at our destination. It was so much fun. When we'd get there, Grams always knew exactly where to go: the thrift store. We would go in, and I would pick out a new hat or outfit for my kids, sometimes having to change their diapers while we were out and about – real diapers, for the record.

Fellow passengers would board behind us at various stops, with some of them stopping to smile and ask me if the dolls were my sisters and brothers. To which I would quickly respond, "They're my kids."

Grams would simply smile back at them. She always supported me, with my kids and all.

Then, we'd go to Govatos Chocolates in downtown Wilmington for our special rice pudding treat, one more Grams-filled and fueled tradition that I couldn't get enough of.

When I was with her during the summer, Grams would take me swimming every single day at Arundel. We made so many friends there. She would always warn me about sunscreen, and I would say, "I know, Grams." I do wish I would have listened a little more. Maybe if I had, I wouldn't have gotten skin cancer at 21.

Altogether, the times I spent with Grams were such special memories that I'll never forget. I did often feel bad that I was having fun while my brother was not. Why couldn't he be there, too? It seemed like such a shame, and it definitely was. Yet Grams made everything seem so much better when it was such a very hard time for my family.

There's so much I could write about my childhood, most of them wonderful memories, especially after Davey came back home, cancer-free – like jamming to Dad's Doo-Wop on his silver old-school radio. There was a tape player in it because he was recording his classic "oldies."

He'd say, "Oopie, listen to this one," and I would. Sometimes I had heard "that one" song a million times. They never got old as we sat together and listened.

Oftentimes, that dinner would be spaghetti and clam sauce. Let's just say that was not my favorite. I think it may be why I still don't like pasta... definitely not with clam sauce.

That strange combination aside, Dad – the "Duke of Delaware" – is where my love of oldies music came from. He also inspired my love of travel, as he was always planning a trip somewhere, mapping out adventures along the way. From road trips to train trips or plane trips, while we were on one escapade, he'd constantly be thinking about where we would be going next, just like I do now.

He especially loved trains. He always talked about them. So, Mom would get everything ready for us, and we would be off.

Some of the best memories I have were on some of those special family adventures.

I remember one time Dad wanted to go to Shell Island in Wrightsville Beach, North Carolina. It sounded so exciting: the thought of seashells everywhere! That's what we thought we'd find, that is.

Mom and I always loved walking on the beach together, and so we did precisely that this time, too. We walked and walked and walked some more on Shell Island, yet never saw a single shell. We couldn't believe it, but we loved every second of the experience anyway.

Another fun adventure I remember was when we took Grams to Gatlinburg, Tennessee. We stayed in a gorgeous cabin with a spiral staircase that went up to a loft with beautiful views of the mountain. There was also a spectacular wooden gondola we got to go on that traveled through the air. It gave us breathtaking views of the snowcapped mountains around us with the surrounding clouds creating such a serene view.

That's to say nothing of the whirlpool there, or the swimming in general. I was a fish, so I loved the water, particularly when I got to combine water with spending time with my adored family.

That was a trip to remember. Though one of the best of all time was our vacation in Jamaica. My whole family went to Dunn's River Falls, where we climbed the falls, snapping pictures at every moment and wading into the water, which was so clear. We went snorkeling, too.

Admittedly, I remember that was also my first time getting seasick. We took the tour boat far out into the deep blue sea with the biggest and slowest waves I have seen and felt. My stomach felt like it was slowly turning with each new crest and dip.

It sure was worth it once we got to where we were going. When we jumped out, we witnessed the most magnificent coral with bright, vivid colors of orange and turquoise. Our guide said over and over again to be careful around it. "It's sharp," he warned us. "Make sure to stay clear."

Of course, what did I do? I cut my foot on the coral. He was clearly right, but I guess I just needed to find that out for myself.

Despite feeling sick and getting scraped, I saw some of the most beautiful tropical fish that day. I don't think I'll ever forget it.

I definitely don't want to.

Growing up, no matter where we went or what we did, I never wanted to disappoint my mom. I always had this deep admiration for her: She reminded me of a saint, and I know I wasn't the only person who thought that. My brother felt so, too. Actually, my whole family thought that. Mom always did everything right.

She always preached about "balance" to me. In fact, she still does. Even when I failed to achieve any such thing, she never failed to be proud of me. Even when I made mistakes – which there were many of – she always helped me learn from them.

Mom is the woman who never ever missed a thank-you, Christmas, or birthday card for anyone in our entire family or all our friends. Everyone loves and respects her so much, including at DuPont where she worked for 51 years. I knew how hard she worked there and how well respected she was. She had started when she was 17 years old and moved her way up the corporate ladder, providing for our family most of that time.

Her love for us was so profound. You could just feel it in your bones. I was always struck by how kind she was to everyone she met, as well. That was just who she was back then and still is today.

I also have to mention St. Catherine of Sienna again. It truly was the perfect school for me despite, or perhaps because, it was small. I'm not sure, but I had an amazing experience there, nonetheless. I had the best of friends there: Beth, Shelly, Nicola, Toby, and Mike, my "boyfriend" for the first two grades. From third grade on, I'll admit I fell in "love" with a new boy in my class every year – Matt, John, Louis… the list went on. I think that's just what you did in grade school.

Then there was my best friend, Joey. We'd call each other "sweeters" even though we were never a couple, talking on the phone until 4:00 a.m. somedays and laughing and laughing so much. He lived in Faulkland Heights in Wilmington, so I would ride my bike there from my neighborhood in Newark – about a 13-mile roundtrip – just to play basketball at the courts.

I'm a social butterfly. That's always who I've been, looking to welcome others wherever I could. However, about my eighth-grade year, I was bullied pretty intensely by two girls in my class. I never really understood why they didn't like me, but they definitely didn't. In hindsight, I think it just became a power trip.

They were always threatening to hurt me, but one time especially stands out. It was an evening I went to the Christiana Mall with my mom, splitting up with the plan to meet back up at a certain time.

As I was walking around, I saw the girls with their two boyfriends. One had a short blonde buzzcut and a big leather jacket, and he just looked like trouble. The second I saw them, I tried to look discreet, hoping they wouldn't see me. I had my head down, walked briskly, and tried to hide behind the person in front of me.

It didn't matter. They saw me anyway and started making fun of me right away. They somehow knew I was with my mom that night, which they thought was hysterical.

I never wanted to fight back; they scared me too much, for good reason, too. The one with the leather jacket opened his jacket to reveal a shiny metal knife, which he proceeded to mention while threatening me.

Petrified, I began to cry and ran off to find Mom. When I found her, with tears flowing down my face, she was furious. All I wanted was to get out of there as soon as possible, but she wanted to do something about it.

"Arianne, this has got to stop."

"No!" I sobbed. "Mom, you can't say anything. You just can't. I don't know what they'll do."

The rest of the school year went on, with high school right around the corner. I never did report them, and I never did fight back. At least I knew I could always look myself in the mirror after everything was said and done, knowing I ultimately carried myself like my mom would want me to. Although it wasn't easy, I do think I was a better person for it.

To stay sane throughout that drama, I reminded myself of the great friends I had. Fortunately, I was captain of my basketball, volleyball, and softball teams, and we brought home several championships that year. Speaking of basketball, I played Stormin' Norman, a basketball league created in 1980, designed to unite Wilmington's community during a time of crime and financial hardship for many living in and around the area. I was on an Amateur Athletic Union (AAU) traveling basketball team, too. My goal was to get a spot on the St. Mark's high school team, and I went for it with everything I had.

I'm not sure if I knew how to do anything else.

3

Learning About Addiction

*H*igh school itself was a blast – definitely not a repeat of eighth grade. The education was great at St. Mark's High School, the teachers were passionate, and the sports were competitive.

I also had a great core group of friends: Jenny Connell, Allison Smith, Kristen McNesby, and Stacey Fahey. We sat together every day at lunch, with Allison getting a hamburger and French fries every single time. We would all tease her for it, but it wasn't like we wouldn't all get the Chipwich – delicious vanilla ice cream between two chocolate chip cookies – every time we could.

I guess when you like a food, you like a food.

I decided to run track my first year at St. Mark's, which I ended up feeling less enthusiastic about than I thought. Other than that, my focus remained on basketball. St. Mark's was pretty darn competitive in that area, but I did make the JV team as a freshman; and then to varsity after that.

I loved being part of such a great team, with so many gifted players. I ended up sitting on the bench most of the time by my senior year. It made me wonder more than once what I was even doing there when I could be playing pick-up ball with my guy friends instead. Ultimately, that was another life lesson – a challenging one, for sure, but a good one nonetheless.

My mom would rent a house for a week in Cape May, New Jersey, during the summers, and Allison would come with me. We had so much fun going to lifeguard parties together, strolling the beach, playing paddleboard…

Then there was that one time where I told her, "I really want to get my belly button pierced."

"Sure." She was all in. "We can do that. I'm older, so I'll just act like I'm your legal guardian."

"Perfect."

So there we went, cruising to Wildwood to get my belly button pierced, hoping my mom wouldn't notice. We must have planned it just perfectly because she never did find out—at least at that time. Our bathing suit time was over for the week, so we went back to Delaware with my new belly button ring, and Mom completely unaware.

When it came to Jenny Connell, she and I just clicked when we met. Two peas in a pod. We would laugh about everything. Except for one time when I happened to be going through some things at home, and I mentioned to her that my dad drank. That's when we found out we had even more in common.

"My dad does, too," she told me. "He's an alcoholic."

I didn't even really know what an alcoholic was, especially since I had just found out the real deal about Santa Claus and the Easter Bunny. Maybe I always seemed to have some kind of blinders on.

I loved those blinders. They seemed to perpetually make everything okay.

"You should come with me to Al-Anon," she added.

"Okay." I was in. "I definitely will." My blinders, I suppose, weren't working so well that day. "What is it, and where is it?"

"It's a group that offers emotional support and resources for people who have an addicted loved one."

I trusted Jenny. Truthfully, I would have done anything she said. So we went that Tuesday afternoon, despite how I had no idea what to expect.

The lady who ran the session was older with light gray hair and had a welcoming approach.

"Tell me what's going on," she prompted me.

"I think my dad is an alcoholic." It hurt to hear the words come out.

"Why do you say that?"

"He drinks all the time. More on Tuesdays. And he and my mom have been fighting quite a bit."

She listened attentively with her fist under her chin as she leaned in, making me feel as at ease as I could be in that painful situation. Then she went on to educate me about alcoholism, including how it was a disease, and one of the ways I could cope with it being in my family she proceeded to share the Serenity Prayer with me:

"God grant me the serenity to accept the things I cannot change, courage to change the things I can, and the wisdom to know the difference."

I repeated it aloud, realizing perhaps for the first time that this wasn't my fault. I knew how much my dad loved me, but I also knew how frustrating and hurtful this was for me to go through.

The people in my life that I loved with all my heart were being consumed by this horrible affliction. I now at least realized that I didn't have to deal with it alone any more than Jenny did. We could address it together.

That was a good thing, considering that I began to notice how irritated I would get whenever Dad started drinking too much. My mom would argue with him more, and Davey would get angry. It just seemed like a vicious cycle.

Things began to escalate further at home until Mom informed me she and Dad were getting a divorce. I remember feeling heartbroken but relieved at the same time. It would be nice, at least, to have less fighting to listen to.

Through all this, searching for some kind of distraction, I began to surround myself with the wrong crowd. It was a group of people who were all older than me; and while they did take me under their wing, I wasn't always making the best choices. That's for sure.

I remember one huge wake-up call was when I was at a party with Jenny and some of our crew. They offered to take me home that night since I'd had a few drinks and some of the others who had come with me had drinks, too. Aaron was safe to drive; if it hadn't been for the other car.

I'll never forget how we were driving down McKennan's Church Road right before the driving range. Just after we passed through the traffic light there, I saw headlights coming fast into our lane. Before I knew it, my head was flying into the windshield since I didn't have my seatbelt on.

It happened right in front of a very nice couple's house, and they came out to call the police and make sure we were all okay. Since I was bleeding a lot, they also called the paramedics.

The woman especially was so kind and encouraged me to call my parents, which was something I did not want to do. I remember having a hard time catching my breath because I was so scared and crying so hard. I think I was in shock, too, when I finally dialed home.

"Mom, it's me. I was in an accident, but I'm okay."

That's honestly the last thing I remember before my mom and brother came to the emergency room, where I was lying on a stretcher. At that point, I was less worried about my health and more worried that I had disappointed them.

Mom wanted me to go to a counselor after that, fully recognizing that the divorce and everything that had led up to it was affecting me. It was a concept I resisted intensely at first though, maintaining that I didn't want to go and didn't need to go, either. However, I finally caved in enough to agree — with a somewhat negative attitude about it on the subsequent drive to Hockessin, mind you. I was feeling very annoyed that she was taking me there.

For the record, I hadn't even told her I was going to Al-Anon. There was clearly a lot I was keeping to myself. Honestly, I really didn't know what I was doing, or feeling, for that matter, as I sat down in the psychologist's office that day.

"Hi, Arianne. Your mom told me what's been going on," she began. "Would you like to tell me how you've been handling all of this? I'm sure it's been very difficult for you."

I wasn't the most receptive, to say the least. "I'm fine."

"Well, she mentioned that she was very worried about you getting in the car when your dad had been drinking."

"It's totally fine. My dad is a professional drunk driver," was my confident response. I meant it, too.

My mom and I laugh about that comment today; about what that nice lady must have thought after those words came out of my mouth. I was old enough to know better, of course. Then again, my glass always seemed to be half-full.

Another way of putting it, I suppose, would be to call me naïve.

4

Summer of '98

I couldn't wait for the summer of 1998! After almost a year of planning our post-senior year experience, my friends and I were setting out to have the best summer of our lives. Dewey Beach, Delaware, here we come!

Graduating high school felt like the best feeling in the world and gave me this sense of freedom. Also, to think I was going to be living with the greatest group of people ever sounded incredible. Allison, Kristen McNesby, Michelle, Megan, Degs, Julie, Jodi, Jenny, Richie, and I were quite the crew, each bringing our own unique energy to the place we rented at 105 Swedes Street Rear.

Despite so many people all living in what was far from a mansion, our house was relatively drama-free. It was definitely full of fun. In fact, we were the place everyone wanted to come to party. Admittedly, that could have also been because we were always stocked with beer and pizza; or because of all the cute girls staying there.

Speaking of such, when it came to safety, we knew Richie, the big brother of the house, always had our backs. Initially, we were so undecided about whether to have him live with us, but we desperately needed a full-timer. Little did we know when we made up our minds that he would be the rock that held us together. Even though he had a tough exterior with his dark, Italian complexion and facial hair, he was so caring and always watching out for us, even when we didn't think he was.

Then there was Allison, who was the designated mother of the house. Since she was 18, she not only signed the lease but also collected all the money and made sure our bills were paid. Despite the whole belly button ring escapade, she really was so responsible. I'm not sure we would have survived otherwise. Allison was so devoted: always a true best friend, no matter what happened.

Her friend, Megan, was one of the sweetest people you would ever meet. She was so quiet compared to the rest of us, but she had this kind way about her and always the cutest giggle, a definite positive addition to our living space.

Kristin Degnars, meanwhile – otherwise known as Degs – still laughs with me to this day about how I didn't like her at first and she didn't like me. We both vaguely remember it being about some boy, Andre. Our taste in music differed too since I grew up playing sports and she grew up in a musical family. Really, everything about us was different. Yet we managed to get past all that to form a friendship that would last forever.

She was only a weekender, but she definitely made her mark. From Allison yelling at her to pay her rent to her leaving her clothes everywhere, we never forgot her. We couldn't. There is only one Degs, and I love her to death.

Kristen McNesby, nicknamed "Smokey," is my second cousin. We grew up together and went to grade school and high school together. So I already knew she was a spitfire. We had such a blast together in high school, including "almost" getting in trouble a few times.

Jenn Cooper, for her part, was hysterical: a wild-woman, you could say. She always had a spirited attitude that made for lots of laughs in our house and she was definitely someone you wanted to party with. She would never let you down for a fun night out in Dewey.

Michelle, or "Toby," and I were best friends in St. Catherine's. We spent eight years together playing basketball, volleyball, and softball and having regular sleepovers. Toby was so beautiful and had such a commanding presence when she entered any room. I felt like she was a little bit of a protector in some ways, too.

She also played with me on that AAU basketball team. We spent so many weekends traveling to tournaments, with our two crazy dads cheering in the stands. She was right there with me again, with her dark-skinned, sun-kissed glow getting darker and darker as the days went on. She was always at the beach sunbathing.

Jodi, very petite with bleach-blonde hair, was adorable in every sense of the word. You could say she was very innocent and naïve, which sometimes made her the brunt of jokes. Nevertheless, she was such a sweet soul who we all loved.

Julie, a weekender, was another friend of Allison's and very motherlike. She had such a beautiful smile and the best laugh to go with it. She also had such a big heart and was so good to everyone.

Then, last but not least, there was Jenny, who I was just as tight as ever with. She would borrow from a popular song at the time to say, "Who the heck is Arianne? What happened to your mother?" and we would laugh for hours on end. We even thought we looked alike, though most people didn't think so at all.

I don't know how many times I told her how beautiful she was. Every time I did, she would consistently respond with, "Oh, Ari-bear, I love you." In which case, the feeling was mutual.

There were so many beautiful connections among us, really making 105 Swedes Street the place to be. Our house was always full of full-timers, weekenders, and random invited and uninvited guests. We welcomed them all. We partied with them all. We loved every second.

Even without the house though, Dewey Beach was the best. As many great times as we had there, we also made our mark on the town.

Everyone seemed to know us wherever we went, whether to parties, bars, the beach, or our go-to place, Grotto's.

Grotto's served the best pizzas after a night out on the town: mouth-watering, warm, thick-crusted pies with just the right amount of sauce and melted mozzarella cheese. After a night of drinking Natural Light – the only beer we could afford – their pies never tasted so good. One piece was never enough. Two wasn't either. Sometimes it had to be three or four, for me anyway. If my friends left their slices untouched for just a second too long, I would always ask, "Are you going to finish that?"

Normal Dewey life started at about nine o'clock for me. As I rolled out of bed, a little groggy of course and hungry for more Grotto's goodness, I'd beeline over to the leftover pizza. Incidentally, it was just as good that way as freshly ordered.

Everyone else would still be sleeping. Perhaps they just weren't as hungry as I was? Everyone except for Allison, who would have already been up cleaning the mess we made. She was a godsend.

The best part was that she was my roommate. The house had three bedrooms upstairs, with each one shared. She was, without a doubt, the most responsible one in our house, which might have made me a far second? I'm not entirely sure.

Once I was fed, the beach would call my name. I would slather on my tanning oil to properly soak in the rays – despite my grandmom's wishes – and head out in my turquoise bikini with my beach chair and towel for some sun and water. At the time, I loved the sun-kissed look too much.

I know. I know. Not the healthiest move. Believe me, I take the necessary precautions these days now that I'm older and wiser.

Allison understood that urge to enjoy every second of the beach. She'd follow me right down every time. Everyone else could catch up when they caught up.

The radiating sun and a comfortable beach chair coupled with a night out always seemed to put me into a restful sleep. I wouldn't wake up again until the sun's heat really got going.

From there, the lure of the ocean would call Allison and me for a dip into its blue-green waves. Splashing, riding waves, and just cooling off – all were a necessity for the both of us. How could we resist? Though I was usually alone for my following long walks on the beach. It was truly one of my most enjoyable things to do, but I guess the thought of exercise in the dry, hot sun after a night of drinking didn't seem too good to anyone else.

I always enjoyed the excitement of all the beachgoers. Sometimes I would see people I knew along my walk. People would call out my name, "Arianne! Arianne!" Oftentimes I would greet them with a smile, not remember their name, and then come back to ask Allison who they were and how I knew them. I still do that to this day. She always knows. I loved the splash of the water on my legs, the sand on my feet, the ocean breeze in my hair, and the uplifting feeling from simply walking. I always loved to move, no matter how I felt. I probably could have walked forever, but duty called and I'd have to get ready for work.

I'd rush back, grab a quick shower, and put my dress and wedges on for work. Getting dressed up is not my strong suit, but at 17 years of age, I must have enjoyed it at some level. Or maybe it was just a requirement? My, how things change. I walked to work since it was just 10 minutes away. At that point, why bother with transportation? Besides, that meant I got to pass my go-to spots along the way at a more leisurely pace, complete with more and more memories to make me smile.

The walk to work was one of my favorite things to do. I would strut down the streets of Dewey in my sundress, wedges, and pocketbook.

There was Starboard on the right, which was close to our house. They played the best daytime music and served great brunch food.

A few blocks down from Starboard was Bottle and Cork. This is where we went to hear great live music. I loved stopping by to hug one of my dearest buddies, Harvey, one of the bouncers there. He'd always have the biggest smile with a heart of gold. Although he may have been intimidating to some people, to me, he was like a big teddy bear.

Then, of course, there was good ol' Grotto's. As I'd pass by, I'd think to myself, *Don't worry, I'll be seeing you again soon.* Pizza and Dewey went together like peanut butter and jelly.

Some days were hotter than others, and I'd break a little sweat before I got there, especially with my overly tanned skin. Some days, I would trip in my wedges. Nothing major, just enough to make some people laugh along the way. My husband refers to girls tripping in heels as drunk giraffes. Although I wasn't drinking, I am sure it was just as funny.

I worked as a hostess at Crabber's Cove in Ruddertown, which was right next to the Lighthouse and Rusty Rudder on the bay. They had delicious hush puppies and, of course, crabs. I was so lucky to get this job and was able to work full-time to support myself that summer. My shift started at two in the afternoon, but I'd always get there to have my delicious snack: French fries with ketchup and ranch dressing. Once again, no one would believe that now. Well, that's not entirely true. I still do love French fries when I get my hands on them. Again, hardly the healthiest life choice. But boy, was it delicious! It was also great to catch up with the other staff in the breakroom. I was the youngest there, so everyone treated me great, kind of like a little sister. If I had time, I'd cool off by the fan, too. That ensured I wasn't a sweaty mess while I greeted the customers.

Now as great as Crabber's Cove was, don't get me wrong, it probably would have been even more fun if I wasn't employed during summer vacation. There were times that I wished I was walking on the beach, but my shift would fly by and I actually had a lot of fun. Nine o'clock would be there before I knew it. Danielle, my manager, gave me a lot of responsibility, and I wanted to make sure everything ran as smoothly as possible: greeting customers, seating arrangements, helping my coworkers, all with a smile. So, there was no time to watch the clock. I also met so many great people that summer: Kevin, Mike, Elaine, Trish, and even some from Ireland.

Danielle was so awesome. In fact, we developed a great friendship. She recognized my strengths early on and realized that I liked to be productive and had a strong work ethic. She trusted me implicitly. So, she gave me additional responsibilities. At one point, she even made me Manager on Duty. I was extremely grateful to her that she had so much confidence in me. It also made work exciting because there was some diversity in my routine.

All in all, working at Crabber's Cove was great. At the end of our shift, we'd all convene in the back sometimes with some more fries, and sometimes I'd hold out for pizza.

I worked full-time so I could party full-time, living up every moment of that summer that I never wanted to end. There was something every night. Whether it was a party that we heard about, or Tuesdays at Summer House in Rehoboth, or Thursdays at the Lighthouse, there was always something fun to do. Let's just say that at 17 all of us couldn't get into the bars, but some of us could. Again, as my older and wiser self, I realize that it may not have been the best decision. But, I wouldn't take it back for the world. It was like living the dream. No matter what we did, it was almost guaranteed to be a fun way to spend the summer nights for as long as they lasted.

Well, not 100 percent guaranteed. We can have the best laid out plans, living in the moment, and sometimes life throws you a curveball. Sometimes those curveballs are despicable. Sometimes they are bewildering. We don't always get to choose how life happens—a fact I was about to learn the hard way.

5

The Best Laid Plans

Before "summer of '98" began, I used to hang with a group of guys; some of the same guys that I was hanging out with around the time of my parents' divorce. Although they were older than me, which made my brother a little concerned, they always took care of me. We shared one of my favorite passions—basketball. They all lived in and around Wilmington, at a place called Faulkland Heights. I met most of them while playing basketball, and I think they all seemed to appreciate my toughness, not just with basketball.

Well, I couldn't drive at the time, but I was determined to play. Part of me felt like I needed to show up regularly to prove my abilities on the court with all the guys. I wasn't too far off on that. So, I decided to ride my bike. It was a decent distance: over six miles each way along some major roads and hills. Although I'm still not sure why my mom let me do that, I did ride my bike everywhere those days. It took me almost an hour to get there, and then, of course, the challenging ride home after a couple of hours of running the court – intensely, might I add. I loved basketball so much, it was always worth it. I made great friends who loved basketball just as much as I did—shooting hoops, dribbling, passing, defense, all of it.

Basketball was my sport. It was my life. It wasn't because my parents wanted me to play. I truly loved it. I was also pretty good at it. Just like the walks on the beach, basketball called my name. Although I never really had a great jump shot, I played defense like no other. I loved being aggressive, with an intensity that only I could have had. I wanted to be like Mike.

In fact, I was obsessed with Michael Jordan in high school. I even had a life-sized poster of him in my room. I admired his extreme focus and desire to be the best. I, by no means, was the best at basketball, but I tried my best. All the guys respected me for that.

Of course, everyone there had their own transportation because they were a bit older than me, so no bicycles were parked on the side of the court for them. Who knows? Maybe they took a little pity on me.

If there was any pity taken, it was because I was the only girl trying to get chosen in an all-guys pick-up game. I knew when it came time for choosing players that I had to show them what I had. I couldn't be too serious. I couldn't help but laugh if my aggressive defense led me to fall on the uneven court. You can't take yourself too seriously. Well, at least I can't.

No matter how you cut it, they adopted me into their family. We formed a solid bond through the sport I loved so much. Whether we were laughing at my determination to get there, or my aggressive defense, shooting hoops, or chumming around, I felt like we'd be friends forever. We'd even have some deep conversations between games or when we would go to get snacks at the neighborhood's 7-Eleven. They were a great group of guys, and I loved hanging out with them.

At 17, admittedly, I was young and innocent and maybe a little naïve. They were like my big brothers. I knew they always had my back, and I knew I could always count on them whether we were on the court or partying at home.

Back to the summer of '98.

One of the exciting things that was planned for the summer was my first booze cruise. Yes, it's just how it sounds. I'd heard so many great things about this. It left from Dewey, and it was supposed to be rated the best. A few people from Crabber's Cove and my buddy Harvey at the Rusty Rudder had mentioned it.

When I first tried to recruit my Swedes Street House, I wasn't getting any takers. I thought it sounded like a blast: a beautiful boat, live music, drinks, food, all on the water. What isn't to like? Regardless, they weren't having it. So, I knew who to ask. Melissa and I went to high school together, and she was living at the beach at the time, too. She loved going out to the bars and parties, and I thought she would definitely say yes. Sure enough, she did. Moreover, she may have been more excited than me.

The first and most important question: "So, what are you going to wear?" As I mentioned, although I don't like getting dressed up now, I must have at that time. Hard to believe. Melissa always looked cute, so I knew she'd be dressed to the nines.

Getting ready for the evening is really where the excitement starts as a teenage girl. All of my crew would weigh in on our attire, makeup, and shoes and, of course, compliment the finished results. Was it girly? Yes. Was it the best? Yes.

After much deliberation about the best outfit to wear, I picked my go-to little black dress that always made me feel great. It was simple but really cute, with a halter top that showed off my shoulders and a fitted feel that highlighted the rest of me. The girls put their stamp of approval on it, so I knew I was good to go.

I looked in the mirror one last time and smiled. I did really love that dress.

When Melissa and I connected on the streets of Dewey, she walked up in her fitted white dress and heels, with her blonde hair flowing, looking cute as ever. We hugged and could barely contain our excitement for our new adventure.

Melissa and I had ourselves put together, dressed and fed, and were ready to go. However, we weren't ready just yet, because we were also taking her friend Karrie, who was always running late. Otherwise known as "Crazy Karrie," she was either trying to figure out what to wear, arguing with someone, or being dramatic. When she was on the guest list, things took a little longer than anticipated. Once she was out and relaxed, she was a blast. So, we figured it was worth the wait.

Once she arrived in her black strappy dress and her short spiky hair, we had to do what we always did, commemorate the occasion with a group picture. It was an essential item on our checklist. There we were. A group of friends, carefree and living it up in Dewey Beach: our smiles grinning from ear to ear, our hair blowing in the breeze, the sand and ocean behind us. It was pure bliss with not a care in the world.

Now we were off to our designated take-off spot. When we first got on the bus, there were tons of new faces and some familiar ones, all with a similar look of excitement. As everyone gathered together as we awaited to board, some regulars were sharing stories of what to expect. It seemed like a guaranteed great evening. They made us feel so welcome and confirmed why we wanted to come so badly. Although we started as one diverse group, we were all one big crazy group looking forward to having a lot of fun.

When we pulled up to the dock, Melissa, Karrie, and I tried to peek out the window to see the ship. I didn't know what to expect, but when I got my first official look at the ship itself, it looked just like the ones on TV, although smaller of course. We smiled at each other and giggled as we were smashed together in one seat on the bus, practically on each other's laps. It was more fun that way.

Everything about the night seemed perfect. There was a beautiful breeze, the temperature was not too hot, small waves were crashing into the boat, and of course, we all were grinning ear to ear in excitement. This cruise was calling us. We piled out of the bus and noticed a short wait on the dock. No worries, we were soaking it all in.

We were laughing and sharing stories with some people we met on the bus. Then, I happened to notice that just like always, I had to have one fashion faux pas. I'm consistent. I lost my dangling silver earring. Of course I did. The night hadn't even started. Once I told the girls, we were laughing hysterically, mainly because this was not the first time, and definitely wouldn't be the last. Then, I happened to look up and saw some of my basketball buddies by the dock. I was so excited and ran up to them to say hello. I gave them all a big hug. I realized I really missed hanging out and playing basketball with them. I definitely did not expect to see them there. They had decided last minute to rent a house for the weekend and were just checking things out. Unfortunately, they were not going on the cruise, but they were seeing one of their friends off, Tony. They introduced me to him, and he seemed super nice, just like my buddies. He was a good-looking guy, wearing a black polo shirt and khaki shorts.

They were always so protective, just like big brothers, and said, "Make sure to take care of our girl!" My impression of him was that he seemed like a nice enough guy and I probably wouldn't even see him most of the night. We were just about to board, and they said, "Dude, keep our girl safe!" I wouldn't have expected anything else from them. He assured them that he'd do exactly that. Hugs all around and then…

There it was: an attention-grabbing, full-throated honking noise from the water. The horn was officially calling us all aboard. This was our time. We waved goodbye, hurried away, and were swept into the crowd. Let's get this party started.

We were all packed together like sardines trying to walk on a ramp with long vertical wooden planks. The planks were creaking as we walked, but made it seem so fun. The girls and I were joined arm and arm laughing, or should I say giggling, the whole time. About what? We had no idea.

There was a man dressed in all black with a captain hat at the end of the ramp who was greeting everyone. He seemed so friendly and confident. Exactly what we want in a captain, of course the latter being the most important.

I was so impressed. We all were. From before we even committed to going to the cruise, to the group picture, and now actually stepping on the boat, it had been so exciting.

Now my excitement had reached its peak. It skyrocketed. It simply couldn't go any higher from there.

Over to the right, I could see the bar and noticed some of my all-time favorites. You guessed it. French fries. I couldn't quite see what they were served with, but it smelled pretty amazing. I'm thinking it must have been burgers. The French fries had me at hello.

But, first things first. To the bar. We already lost Karrie. She always was a social butterfly. So, she was off mingling and checking things out. It was likely that we may not see her again, but everyone seemed so nice, so that wasn't a problem. We never got mad at each other for that, as long as we were all having fun. Melissa and I beelined over to the bar. Great minds think alike. She managed to get her cranberry and vodka first, as she always did, and we had to wait a few extra minutes to get my vodka and tonic.

We laughed and hugged, taking it all in while we waited for our drinks.

Then, after several sips in, we decided to take our first official on-the-cruise picture of the evening. We had to get the pictures early in the evening: One, so we looked our freshest and two, so we didn't forget. We had to officially document our first booze cruise.

"Melissa! Melissa!" I yelled as I grabbed her away from the bar while she was getting her second drink. I just heard the first couple of tunes and I knew – there it was, the best song of the summer of '98. As I made my way to the dance floor, dragging Melissa's arm, "Ghetto Superstar" by Mya came on full blast. She could wait for her drink; this girl had to dance.

"Ghetto Superstar" was a super popular song and was played regularly in our Swedes Street household. We would turn that song up so loud whenever it came on the radio, and we would jam out to it, singing, laughing, and dancing like crazy.

My roomies would inevitably make fun of my dance moves in the process, and with good reason. At that time, I would be the first person to admit that there was definitely something missing in my dance moves, particularly, rhythm. Rather, I had the entertaining "mom dance." In essence, that is, in case you are wondering, three main moves—step, snap, and clap.

Then repeat.

After my song was over, there was another great hit. And another. And then another. Each one was better and better, and before you knew it, we were cuttin' a rug on the dance floor. The night was flying by. It was already nine o'clock.

Somewhere between Montell Jordan's "This Is How We Do It," and Naughty by Nature's "O.P.P." I noticed a tall, strong, handsome guy standing over my shoulder. I knew he was watching me, and the first thing that went through my head was *I'm not looking for a date, buddy. I'm just having fun with my friends.*

Before I was filled with aggravation, I realized it was Tony, my friends' friend. "Hey, Tony!" I yelled. He smiled back. I realized he was just doing what my friends had asked him to do. He just checked in, made sure I was okay, and when he realized there was nothing to worry about, he moved on. That was nice, I thought.

Although the dance party was a blast, we did leave the floor occasionally to take in everything. Staring out into the water at night was nothing short of spectacular. We wandered around the boat several times and each spot was a whole new experience.

After roaming around, we finally made our way up to the second floor, where we enjoyed an even more beautiful view, if that was possible. There were quite a few other people up on the top deck. They had the same idea. We all enjoyed the music, the views, the dancing, and the company.

Admittedly, our feet were a little tired and worn, especially in our wedges. Let's just say this: they were definitely made for style, not function. We made our way to a seat and ended up sitting next to the nicest girls who, as it turned out, lived right up the street from us.

After a bit of chatting with them, and of course, some more laughter and group pictures, Melissa and I realized our hunger was taking over. We made our way back to the food for some of those French fries that smelled so delicious when we came on board. When we saw the table, most of the food had been devoured. There was just enough left for the two of us to get an adequate amount.

Taking our small, but adequate, food with us, we headed over to the side of the boat for some more much-needed foot rest. There we were, fueled and armed for continued fun.

I saw Tony walking over to check on us again, at least that is what it seemed. He asked how we were doing and if we needed anything. Despite us likely not looking how we did when we got there, perhaps a bit more tired and disheveled, we were, of course, doing great. We assured him we needed a quick break and we'll be back on the dance floor before we knew it. He stuck around for a few minutes, so he may have needed a break, too.

I couldn't help but notice that he had spilled ketchup all over his shirt. As I always do, I started laughing hysterically and teasing him. It's absolutely something I would do; however, he didn't need to know that. He laughed at my observation, agreeing: "Yes, I sure did."

Though we had plans to get back out on the dance floor, Melissa and I were whooped. We didn't budge from then on. Karrie was nowhere to be found. Then again, we didn't actually look for her. Tony went back to doing his own thing. We just sat and chatted quietly.

Then, the boat eased into its dock space, and Melissa and I pulled ourselves up from the extremely comfortable bench and began to walk down the ramp to the bus stop. It was finally time to go home, or so we thought. Even though we were dragging our feet a bit, literally, we realized everyone seemed to have a lot of energy. We couldn't imagine how. Yet we climbed the bus steps, found our seats, and noticed the same level of energy and excitement as the ride there. This time there may have been a bit more alcohol consumed, however. So, everyone was a bit louder and funnier.

As we listened to everyone's plans, the lifeguard party seemed to be the ticket. They had a reputation for throwing great parties, from what I had heard. So, it was definitely tempting to go. We also reasoned that we were nicely rested from all of our downtime. Right?

It didn't take long for us to decide we were in. Bring it on. We are young and free. Why not? We have no curfew and nothing to worry about.

When we arrived, everyone piled out of the bus. Not everyone went, but a large majority of the group did.

Looking from the outside, the house looked just fine. Well, better than fine. It looked like it was going to be incredibly fun. There were lots of people in the back, some music playing, and kegs that I could see. There were no "Danger" or "Keep Out" signs to be seen. No ominous-looking men lurking behind trees. Our women's intuition never kicked in to tell us this wasn't going to be safe.

It seemed like almost everyone was there, a booze cruise reunion. It was so inviting.

As I stepped into the house, I had three priorities, with number two and three being a close tie. It didn't matter if I found the drinks or the dance floor first, I was ready.

Priority one, however, was most definitely priority one. That meant a quick trip to the ladies' room, as was customary for me whenever I entered a new building. I think everyone close to me always says, "Arianne, you have to pee AGAIN?"

One of the lifeguards, someone I'd met earlier in the summer, was kind enough to show me the way. He probably didn't remember, but I was pretty sure he'd been the one who blew his whistle at me a few weeks ago after I got too close to the rope line. No big deal though. He was just doing his job.

As I cut down the small hallway, I passed a girl I knew from high school.

"Hey, Megan! I would chat, but I gotta run. Know what I mean?"

She laughed and said, "No worries, I'll catch up with you later." I felt bad, but I figured I'd just be a minute, and I assured her I'd find her afterward.

I meant it too. I had no intention of blowing her off, and I wouldn't have, if left to my own devices. It was just that someone else had other intentions that changed everything about that night, and so much after it.

I finally made it. The bathroom was so small, and it was not the most pleasant. Considering a bunch of dudes lived there, that was to be expected, I guess. When I was washing my hands, I heard Lauryn Hill's "Killing Me Softly."

I smiled and thought, *I could even mom-dance to this. You can mom-dance to anything. You just speed up or slow down the tempo. I wonder if Megan would be up for catching up on the dance floor, or should we say backyard?*

As I opened the door, I thought she may still be there, but there was no sign of her. Then, I felt someone grab my left arm and pull me in the direction opposite to the one I intended to go.

For a quick second, I thought it was Melissa telling me we needed to go until I felt pain in my arm. It wasn't a friend, and there was nothing about that touch that was familiar or comfortable.

I felt disoriented and scared for a moment as I didn't realize who was grabbing me aggressively and why. I still instinctively tried to pull away and said, "Get off me!" My panic-stricken bug eyes finally caught a glimpse. It was Tony. The same Tony who'd promised my friends to look after me. Who had seemed so very pleasant and protective and friendly back on the cruise. It was Tony.

It didn't make sense. Why was he so aggressive? He seemed so nice.

What was he even saying? Was he even saying anything?

Maybe I could have figured it out if I just had a moment to compose myself. If I had a moment to breathe. If I had a moment to collect my thoughts. But that didn't happen. It couldn't happen.

He was hostile and demanding to the point where I was seriously disoriented in those first few crucial seconds. Seconds. That's all it was, I believe. It felt like minutes.

While I was still trying to process all of that, there was an intense punch-like pain on my shoulder as he threw me into the room. The room right next to the bathroom. I saw it when I ran by. Megan was standing there before I went in. I remembered it.

I didn't understand what he was doing. I just wanted him to stop hurting me already.

What had I done to make him act like that? Why was he so violent? He was so pleasant earlier.

The deeper answer to that question would take an eternity to figure out. As for the immediate answer, he trapped me in the room with him, locked the door, and was staring me right in my terrified face. He started pulling at my clothes, so despite my panic, I quickly realized what his motives were.

Immediately, I began screaming at him to stop. I realized running out of there was not an option, so I fought him with all the strength I had in my body. But he was just too powerful. Just too large. Just too aggressive.

Just too intentional. Whether he'd planned it out from our first introduction or whether he'd spotted me walking to the bathroom alone and decided on his course of action then, he clearly knew what he wanted, what to do, and how to do it.

Unlike me. All I could do was react. I never thought something like this could happen. I didn't know what to do.

"Get off of me! Get off of me!" I screamed over and over again.

I fought back as much as I could, but he made sure that I wasn't going far. With his strong arms holding me down and his knee holding my leg, I tried desperately to get out and get away. No matter how I tried to escape, it felt like I kept getting weaker and he kept getting stronger.

Why can't he see the pain on my face?

Why won't he let me go?

I could feel the firmness under his pants.

How can he? How can he do this?

But he was.

Just look at my face. Look what you are doing to me. This isn't right.

He didn't care. No matter how hard I resisted, he didn't care. Because despite all my intensely desperate efforts, he took what he'd come for. Something no other man had taken at that point in my life.

When he was finished, he relaxed for a long enough moment that I finally got my opportunity to escape. I fled the house, running down the street, crying and crying. I had an overwhelming sense of disbelief about what had happened in that room. I didn't know what to do.

I was alone.

I was scared.

I was embarrassed.

I was disgusted.

I didn't want to interact with anyone. I didn't want to look at anyone or have anyone look at me. I just wanted to get away. I made my way to our beach house alone, with the ocean waves as my only company. I remember the stillness of the night like it was yesterday. It seemed like all I could do was replay the sounds of him yelling, the sensation of him pulling my arm and throwing me on the bed, the smell of his cologne. All of it. Every last detail, over and over and over again.

I remember a thousand questions running through my mind, with only a few answers following behind.

When I got home, I knew I needed to be alone. I wandered around the house to find a spot. This was the only thing I was certain about right now, that I needed time. What I would do when I got there was far beyond me as I searched; all I knew was that I needed to be by myself. That was it.

Fortunately, Allison wasn't there, and so I went to my bedroom, away from the windows, in a dark corner where I could sit alone. That's when I realized that it wasn't a mere desire to be alone that I'd been searching for: it was a desire to hide. I not only wanted to hide, but I needed to hide. I needed it so bad. I wanted it all to go away.

Did this really happen?

The tears were rolling down my face. I couldn't even control them. I felt numb. I wanted to hide forever. Even from myself. How could this happen?

6

Life Goes On

Just like they say, life goes on. So, it did right after the most horrific thing that has ever happened to me. I realized that when I woke up the next morning. There was no going back to undo anything. It was forward or nothing.

That day, I skipped the leftover pizza. I didn't go to the beach either. I guess I wasn't feeling any of that. I did get dressed and go to work.

I didn't tell anyone what had happened. Not my roommates. Not my coworkers. Not my family: not even Mom, whom I trusted more than anyone in the world. Absolutely no one.

Perhaps people could tell I wasn't myself? Or maybe not. I'll admit that I probably took "life goes on" to a new level, and not just intentionally leaving everyone in the dark like that. What was I supposed to do? I had to pick up my bootstraps and move on. Right?

I thought that, if anyone, Melissa might have asked what happened to me. Although, life went on for her, too, and so she never did. I don't blame her for it. How would she know anything like that could have happened? Besides, my sudden departure from the party wasn't all that odd. It wasn't unlike me to just leave when I was ready.

As more time went on, I did find that there was more and more normalcy I could rely on. I laughed with my roommates again. I even started getting hungry for leftover Grotto's pizza again. I got thirsty, too.

Yet even though some things seemed normal, I wasn't. I wasn't the same person, I knew, and would find myself lost in deep seas of serious self-reflection on an all-too-frequent basis, fixated on unanswerable questions.

Did I have too much to drink that night?

Did I lead him on in any way?

Did he think I was flirting with him?

Should I not have worn my cute, black dress?

These questions, and so many others, dominated my thoughts when I was alone. I couldn't get away from them. If I kept asking, perhaps I would get some answers?

That was all on the inside. On the outside, I was still the same ol' silly and fun-loving Arianne. I chose to stay silent because I refused to give Tony or what he had done to me any power.

At least that is what I told myself. In all honesty, I think I was simply too terrified to tell anyone, even Mom, the sweetest and most loving person in my world. At 17 years old, still dealing with irrational and immature thinking, I felt as if I'd disappointed her with what had happened. As if I had a choice. As if I'd given consent.

I know my mom wouldn't have been any different than the most caring, loving, and supportive parent that she always is. But at the time, I truly wasn't in my right mind. I could barely process what had happened, and I thought in some ways I could pretend that it didn't happen. I could make it go away.

This was supposed to be the summer of a lifetime, spent with best friends I loved so much. The thought of dwelling on anything else and ruining the summer seemed too wrong. Too painful.

Telling myself that I wouldn't let anything – even that – affect my friends, family, or summer in any way, I began throwing myself into those days more and more. I became unstoppable, it felt, as did everyone else. Our Swedes Street house continued to make so many great memories and lots of laughter. We'd walk down the streets of Dewey like we were famous, waving and visiting people all over, getting enthusiastic welcomes from whoever we saw.

Better yet, with each week that passed, our bond became so much stronger. Yes, we'd started out close. Some of us were even very close. Our connections kept strengthening with every new experience we shared.

We were all so unique, from our personalities to our qualities, strengths, and, shall we say, tendencies. Admittedly, the weekenders were messy. There were very few Mondays that went by that Allison and I didn't say, "Gosh, the weekenders are so messy." If it wasn't that, we'd talk about whoever didn't pay their part of the rent on time. Yet despite our differences and aspirations, with some of us collegebound and some set to seek jobs after the summer ended, we all had one thing in common: We were going to live it up every single summer night.

Even me.

Eventually, our time on Swedes Street came to an end, still with no answers to those questions I couldn't always ignore. It was probably a good thing then that I had to change gears and direct my attention toward starting my freshman fall semester at the University of Delaware. I'd been looking forward to this since I got accepted.

Back at St. Mark's, I had volunteered with Blue & Gold and Special Olympics, experiences that helped me determine exactly what I wanted to do academically. I got involved in the first place because of one of my teachers and mentors, who I'll never forget, Mr. Tony Glenn. He was so inspiring to me: the most genuine and sincere man you could ever hope to meet. Somehow, he always saw something in me that I didn't really understand, but mattered so much to me anyway.

He encouraged me to pursue volunteer experiences and since I respected everything he said, I also volunteered with a physical therapist who worked with children with disabilities. It turned out to be an even more rewarding experience than the Special Olympics. It seemed like the perfect fit for my interests and gifts, taking what I'd learned from Mr. Glenn to a whole new level.

I had loved every second of it. My mentor's knowledge and passion for what she did was truly changing these families' lives. The children we worked with were so special, and I quickly realized how much we take for granted, including the ability to move. That's when I knew I wanted to be a physical therapist.

It was an obvious decision.

That meant I applied to the University of Delaware as a "pre-PT," or biology, major. That is how I was accepted, ready to soak up all the knowledge I could for my career planning.

Of course, I easily could have lived at home. I did live only 10 minutes away. But like most freshmen, I'd already decided long ago that I was going to live on campus. I had to work up to three jobs at one point to pay for it, but it was well worth it. There were countless perks, with the best one being my amazing roommates, Leah and Rachelle. I'd already corresponded with Rachelle by the time I packed up all my things from 46 Willow Creek Lane, where I'd been for the past 10 years. I knew Leah from high school. So, I wasn't worried about any conflicts between us.

Mom and Dad both helped me load up the car for my new stage in life, which was typical for them. However, the ride there wasn't as exciting as I had hoped. My parents were not on the best terms, and so there was a noticeable tension in the air. Their relationship was considerably strained at this point.

Fortunately, my dad's Doo-Wop made things seem a little lighter. I have to say that they always managed to pull it together for me, ultimately making it a memorable and enjoyable day. We brought my boxes and mini-fridge into the new dorm, walked around campus, and mingled with my new roomies.

As I said, I already knew Leah. We'd even done a school project together for a theology class, which turned out to be an entertaining experience that we'd never forget. As I recall, it was a group project, and we all headed over to her house to make the video we'd decided on. It was a great experience, filled with confusion and corresponding laughter as we pieced everything together.

I don't remember what grade we got on the final product. But, for the two of us, it was all we needed to form a solid connection. When she walked in with her brown curly hair and a big smile, I knew nothing had changed in that regard.

Rachelle, meanwhile, was from the D.C. area, assigned to us by luck of the draw. We'd talked over the phone more than once that summer as we got to know each other and figured out what we would need and not need for college life. When we met face to face on move-in day, there were no evil surprises there. She turned out to be just as awesome in person as she was a hundred and fiftyish miles away.

There was one little incident that happened, however. I had worn this sleeveless tank top that came right down to meet my shorts. So, as I reached up to put a box on top of the closet, it easily came up, showing my belly button ring off, clear as day – right in front of my mom and dad.

I had a bit of explaining to do after that. Fortunately, they didn't see the tattoo I'd gotten over the summer; and I didn't bring it up. I figured we were all better off saving that for another awkward time.

Once we were all moved in, Rachelle quickly took the mom role in our tiny dorm room on Ray Street. She was unbelievably organized and protected anyone she loved, including Leah and me.

That meant setting up rules for the dorm right away, not only to keep things orderly but also to make sure we were always okay. I remember if Leah or I didn't come home when we were supposed to – which was whenever we originally indicated – Rachelle would call to make sure we were okay. It always seemed so loving… until the next morning when she scolded us, as only she could do.

We knew she loved us. We loved her just as much.

Leah and I seemed to be on the same page with how we approached college. There were two goals we had: One, have a lot of fun. Two, learn. In that order.

Our dorm was close to everything. So, while in the beginning, we didn't know where all the cool places were just yet, we knew we would soon enough. There was a week-long period before classes began that included orientation and chances to tour the campus, including the Trabant center, food hall, and, of course, the gym.

More than once, I did have to remind myself of the main reason I was there: to learn as much as possible. Or was that reason number two?

I didn't know exactly what to expect when I walked into Room 43D, my very first class on my very first day. I'm sure I didn't expect it to be quite that overwhelming. Although I thought I was ready to dive into the new course material, I found myself a bit taken aback by the enormous lecture hall. There were more than 300 people all in that same class!

It was a far cry from my 25-student spaces at St. Mark's. It sure was much easier to fall asleep that way, lost in the crowd as I was. Though there just may have been a few other factors that played into my unintentional naps as well.

Let's just say that I was quite a social butterfly in college. I wanted to be involved in everything, and so I was. My very long list of extracurricular activities included the obvious college parties several nights a week, meeting friends for lunch, playing sports, going to the gym, and so much more. The parties were always so tempting, even though they never seemed to work well with next-day classes.

There were just so many places to see and people to meet. How could I say no?

Really, there was a lot I did that first semester that didn't jive well with my academic goals. It wasn't just the party scene that I threw myself into with reckless abandon. There were clubs and groups and activities I wanted to explore, too.

I really and truly wanted to be a part of everything.

To some degree, it was about me being me. An extrovert who loves interacting and experiencing all life has to offer, I have an unwavering desire to explore new things. I've been that way my whole life, and I expect I always will.

Admittedly though, there may have been another aspect to all of my busyness that was less nature and more nurture. Because constantly going places and doing things meant I had so much less time to dwell on a certain incident from less than a year ago.

So out and about I went, joining the physical therapy interest club, which I thought would be a great way to get some experience and build my portfolio. I even checked out sorority life, realizing quickly enough that it wasn't for me. It was a huge commitment that meant I would have had to be with the same girls all the time. They seemed nice and all, but I was making friends all over campus and didn't want to be pigeonholed.

Now, what did seem like a perfect fit for me was the intramural basketball team. We played in the school gym right down the street from my dorm, so it made it very manageable, comparatively speaking, to fit it into my already busy schedule.

Then, there was the life-changing experience of Best Buddies. Its website, bestbuddies.org, explains:

Best Buddies International is a nonprofit 501(c)(3) organization dedicated to establishing a global volunteer movement that creates opportunities for one-to-one friendships, integrated employment, and leadership development for people with intellectual and developmental disabilities.

When I first committed to it, I thought I'd be able to make a huge difference in their lives. Little did I know that they would literally change mine as well. I was matched with an amazing woman named Missy Gramaldi who has cerebral palsy and is confined to an electric wheelchair.

The first time I went to the Mary Campbell Center to meet her, we sat and talked for over an hour. When I left that day, I remember feeling this weight lifted from me. She had so many challenges, yet she was the kindest person you could ever meet, a first impression that kept being confirmed as I met with her week after week. Each time, I spent a little over an hour with Missy and other residents.

I also went to their holiday events, even taking Leah with me to their prom one time. We got all dressed up and danced the night away with them in their wheelchairs for a night I'll never forget.

I even started to figure out how to take them out on mini-excursions. I'd coordinate with the Center so they'd have transportation to and from dinner. One time, Missy and her boyfriend, Phil, met me at Friday's restaurant. She ended up accidentally hitting her electric wheelchair in such a way that it elevated her seat, which took the table off the ground and knocked off all the drinks and plates – something we laughed about for months to come.

Best Buddies taught me so much about what true strength is all about. These amazing individuals aren't born with so many of the gifts many of us have, but you wouldn't know it by spending time with them. They get the most out of life every day, finding sunshine in the clouds. And, through adversity, they achieve dignity and purpose that is noteworthy and outright admirable.

The impact the Best Buddies program had on my life was enormous. The people I met there became my friends, my confidants, my inspiration. They still are today. So much of the success I've had in my life has been drawn from the strength they first shared with me.

I don't regret that time spent one bit, but I do fully admit that I should have cut other activities out. Truth be told, I'm still not exactly sure how I fit everything in that I did, especially when I was still working. That included my first job, Cokesbury Village, a retirement community, in Hockessin. This helped me to pay for room and board at UD and it helped even more when I was promoted to a dietetic assistant, which meant more leadership and more compensation.

Obviously, I couldn't walk away from that. Besides, it was the best job ever with a boss I absolutely loved, coworkers who were my friends, and residents who were so kind and welcoming. They could always put a smile on your face no matter what was going on. Pat Hand, my boss, had such a strong influence on my career as a dietitian and was one of my biggest supporters.

The problem was that everything else I did could, and did, bring a smile to my face, too. That's why I didn't give them up. There were so many cherished memories that I wouldn't trade for the world.

Of course, I couldn't keep up that frantic pace. I don't think I would have, if not for the aftereffects of what happened at the lifeguard house. That first semester of college could have been perfect without that pain and guilt, and that terrible feeling that I'd disappointed my mother.

I can't tell you how much I wanted to go back to the moment before it all happened. The moment before my power and strength were taken from me. The moment before my choice was trampled and torn to pieces, and my words meant nothing.

If I just didn't drink so much…

If I didn't wear that dress…

Why didn't I fight harder?

So many questions. So many doubts.

If only I knew then what I know now: that guilt can deplete our physical, emotional, and spiritual energy. That we don't have to bear that shame alone. That we don't have to bear it at all. The 17-year-old version of me let this man have power over me for far too long. The 40-year-old version of me never would have let that happen.

However, since the 17-year-old me didn't yet know what she would one day recognize, I found myself somewhat lost. I was disorganized, and I definitely didn't prioritize schoolwork. That fact slapped me in the face when I received my first grades.

Academic probation?

Me?

As a former straight-A student, I couldn't believe it. My first few months of college completed, and I was failing.

What am I doing? This isn't me.

I remember the psychology test that especially solidified that undesirable outcome. That's how this learning-hungry, driven, and passionate young woman found herself officially on the academic outs.

It shouldn't have happened in a long list of "shouldn't have happened." Yet it did and, fortunately, this one woke me up, helping me visualize my goals and teaching me to change what I needed to.

For somebody like me who could not (or did not) get enough sleep at night, I did find well-attended lectures to be my sweet escape into a deep slumber. The rooms were crowded, and I was lucky enough to hide from the watchful gaze of my early-morning professors.

I knew I shouldn't sleep in psychology class in particular. Although, I found myself doing that more often compared to my other classes; Skipping too, since I came to believe that my absence wouldn't matter.

Despite knowing that a test was coming up, I chose to spend the remaining days before it visiting places and meeting people. When the new week – test week – began, I was fully aware I wasn't even an inch closer to being properly prepared for the Friday exam. Telling myself I had plenty of time left anyway, I spent Tuesday away from my books. And then Wednesday. And then it was Thursday.

There were so many things to do, but I just kept telling myself I was living the college dream. So even on Thursday, I didn't do anything to alleviate my jam-packed day. I went to my classes and participated in my activities and spent my time after that with friends. Going out with them every Thursday night had been a routine for me, and skipping this one would mean alone time for me – something I knew I didn't want.

Perhaps I was afraid of it.

That's how, on Friday morning, I was in a mess and in no way prepared. Not to worry though, I informed myself. It was normal for a college student like me to get a C once in a while. I assured myself that there were worse things in life and that a C wouldn't cloud my whole college life, anyway.

That pep talk didn't work as well as I intended it to though under the realization that a C was not fine at all. Not for me. Not for this class: one I was really interested in where my future was on the line.

Clearly, I wasn't being myself. Skipping classes and worse, ignoring my studies, wasn't like me. Neither was the D I ended up receiving for the whole course.

My final grades that semester were so poor that I didn't want to acknowledge them. One part of me couldn't understand how I ended up hitting rock bottom; the other self understood completely well. It was at that moment when I finally told myself two important realities I'd failed to tell myself before:

This is definitely not me. Surely, this is not what I want for myself.

Fortunately for me, there was a Gold's Gym about 10 minutes from campus that a few of my guy friends were going to. If you know Gold's Gym, it's the real deal, created for people who are serious about getting strong. My friend Rick, who trained there, was proof of that.

It was more accurate to say that he lived there, pumping weights whenever he could.

Conversely, despite being so active in playing sports, I had never done any formal training. Playing basketball, of course, requires a bit of stamina, coordination, and agility; but it's not the same as throwing around some heavy weight.

Despite my lack of experience and the fact that none of my girlfriends were into that kind of thing, there was something very compelling about it that grabbed my attention. I found myself dwelling on all the ways the body can be trained through movement and how it can adapt to physical challenges when given the right education. It seemed like something I could accomplish after such an unsuccessful first semester.

So, after some serious thought and consideration, I finally asked Rick to show me around and give me a basic strength-training program. As any self-respecting weight-training enthusiast would, he agreed to teach me his methods. This meant I learned about the key lifts: deadlifts, chest presses, rows, lunges, and squats. He also taught me some challenging hanging leg raises for my core too, where you engage your abdominals and hip flexors to raise your legs outward in front of you while hanging from a bar. I watched him demonstrate each one, listening attentively and trying to execute them to the best of my ability in turn.

As I did, I felt my body challenged as it had never been before. My muscles were strained as they adapted to the movements and lifts. Yet it was a good experience, even empowering! It felt like I was challenging myself in a very constructive way as opposed to some of the destructive behavior I was getting used to.

It felt like… me, which was a wonderful thing. I didn't realize exactly how much I'd missed, until then.

The deadlift was my favorite exercise. There was something about wrapping my hands around a heavily loaded bar in front of me, taking a big breath in, and forcefully exhaling as I lifted the bar to hip height. It was a feat that made me proud and strong again.

Every rep counted, grounding me physically but also mentally, emotionally, and even spiritually. The experience of learning these new movements gave me this strange but undeniable sense of peace, not to mention a deep connection with and appreciation for the human body and spirit alike. Although it was such hard work, it gave me a new way to relax – something that had seemed almost impossible before.

Each and every time I lifted, my intention was that of all-inclusive strength. It allowed me to tap into a power I didn't even realize I had.

At the very same time and in the best possible way, I felt humbled and overcome by a sense of gratitude for the ability to move, connect, and gain control of my body and life.

After I learned the basics, I began going to the gym regularly – five days a week. I had a great routine and felt stronger each time I went.

Some people might not have understood the importance of the equipment I used. It might not have meant anything to them other than a filthy barbell resting on the floor. Or nothing but a cylindrical piece of metal struck between two weighted disks: something that can easily be forgotten. A powerless, lifeless object.

To me, it was more than that. Those pieces of metals were the end of the agony. They were the turning point against uncertainty, guilt, and the internal confusion twirling inside of me.

They served as channels of finding myself again. I took pleasure in them, and it showed.

It wasn't too long before the gym's owner told me I'd make a great contender for an upcoming fitness competition. Being new to that world, a lot of questions popped up in my mind like: When will the competition be? What preparations do I need to do? How many people will I compete against?

But honestly, as an 18-year-old girl, I just felt privileged. As soon as the words were out of my mouth, I knew from the beginning that my answer would absolutely be a yes.

It looked fairly easy. That's how the gym owner described it: as simple as receiving a weekly nutrition plan and workout regimen. During that period of time, my body fat would also be tested. Always. That's how it would be for the next five months. I would also have to come up with an overall fitness routine, learn how to pose, and meet with a choreographer.

I admit that those last two details were somewhat frightening. All of a sudden, I had this very strong reservation about whether the mom-dance would work. The competition was going to be an arduous battle – an intimidating thought, to be sure.

It was just not intimidating enough for me to say no to such a thrilling opportunity.

For the record, I did think about it for a couple of days. I reflected on everything, from the commitment I had to pledge, the time requirement and obligation it came with, the diet restrictions – including the thought of never having the chance to enjoy the foods I love during the whole process – and everything there was to anticipate. Plus, this time I knew I would have to set aside time to focus on my grades.

I also knew that I worked best when I had goals to meet, unlike how it had been the previous semester. So I carefully thought about what was suitable around my academic drives and what wasn't.

After a couple of days of considering and reflecting, I decided to jump over the hurdle. Wait and see, Miss Fitness America and Miss Figure U.S.A.! Arianne was in the running!

As a result, a lot of changes occurred over the next few months. My whole life completely changed after I inscribed my signature on the dotted line. I had to cut down on my food intake, completely eliminate alcohol from my life, visit the gym five to six days a week, and practice consistently on my choreography.

Looking back, it wasn't like how the gym owner made it look. In reality, it was very different: a huge task, all things considered.

Just like with many other diets, especially extreme ones like mine, I had to limit myself from going to bars, diners, and other sorts of eateries. Time restrictions played a portion of that; but for the most part, it was because I just couldn't consume any food featured in those places. There wasn't even a single salad I could choose from – not even one on a low-fat menu. That's why, when going out with friends, I had to practically prepare my own food and bring it with me.

Not even a single stick of French fries I could casually grab from my friends' plates was allowed to pass through my lips.

Perhaps that was the most challenging part of the training. Not the French fries, but the way the meals were prepared in general. In fact, I sometimes felt like cooking and eating were all-consuming.

It could be a real pain in the neck, but those sacrifices brought me into another important step of realizing who I was and what I was capable of doing. Those bits of sacrifices gave me meaning and helped me decide to put my energy into the bigger picture instead of weakening myself.

Moreover, those little sacrifices made me concentrate on myself.

As my improvement continued, the commitment I made and the great results that came with it got my personal trainer's approval. That intensified all the wonderful thoughts and emotions already pouring through me, fueling me even more. I hadn't realized I was accomplishing my set strength goals every week, so it was great to hear that all my work was paying off.

In no time, I got down to 9% body fat and started to see muscles I didn't realize I had before!

With the new challenges I embraced each day that came along, I gradually saw myself transforming into what I imagined a fitness champ should be. By that, I mean my mind and emotions were sharpening too. My progress made contributed significantly to everything I did and saw.

Who knows? Those challenges might have given me the wisdom to figure out what major I really wanted to pursue, nutrition and dietetics with a fitness concentration. My classes immediately became so much more fun after switching majors as I gained information about the subject matter -- information I could relate to on many levels.

It was obviously the right decision since I made Dean's list my first semester in that major.

Despite those accomplishments, I continued to volunteer for Best Buddies and stayed as close as ever with my friends. Those relationships weren't worth giving up for anything, competition or academic standing or anything else.

Besides, we shared so many laughs together while I was preparing for Miss Fitness America and Miss Figure U.S.A., oftentimes about peanut butter. Back then, I was heavily hooked on the all-American treat.

Truly, I still am, but I was even more so during my college days.

Leah and Rachelle, being completely aware of my diet restrictions, would label all the kitchen cabinets with signs so I wouldn't indulge in that tasty treat in a jar. They would even place signs on the jars themselves, to be absolutely sure.

I'd still delve, but those notes they left behind were highly entertaining anyway. Those moments were what mattered to me so much, as I felt how much support they had for me. They and my other friends and family members would always look out for me, understanding everything I was doing and what I was trying to achieve.

My mom was very worried despite giving me such amazing support. It seemed to her as if I was getting thinner every time, and so she would ask what I'd been doing to get in that state.

I may not have looked healthy in her loving eyes, but I still knew she was proud of me.

I noticed that the workout part of my preparation was doable about one week before the competition. The same did not apply, however, for the diet portion. Honestly, that was the part I found much harder. If anything, it was becoming increasingly more tempting – not less – to give in to certain foods that I was totally restricted from eating.

Except for peanut butter. That was the exception since I kept eating it anyway. I just can't deny how good these ground roasted nuts were.

My perseverance, self-discipline, and intrinsic drive left me feeling immensely satisfied on the day of the competition. Once again, this wasn't just a physical appreciation, but a mental and spiritual one as well.

I had done it! I had achieved what I'd set out to accomplish! Even before the competition had officially begun, I knew I had already earned the real prize I'd been striving for since the beginning.

If I could get through the last few months, what else could I deal with?

The immediate answer, of course, would be the actual Miss Fitness Competition. I'll admit that it was a daunting thought as I got ready for the day. From a mind-body-soul outlook, standing on that stage was already the hardest part of it all.

I knew it wasn't just about posing and being compared with the other participants, despite how the final judgment did come down to who had the fittest body. Behind that, first and foremost, competitors had to be completely educated on several nutrition principles designed to prepare the body on how to endure such arduous training.

Anyone can get through an extremely difficult and concentrated workout regime. However, without securing the proper nutrition to upkeep them, their results will only be somewhere around average.

There's also the extraordinary work ethic involved in coming back for more of the same exercises day in and day out. It's about establishing one resource on top of another and creating a body that can power through. The education alone, not to mention the goal of getting healthy and fit, are hard enough on their own. Combining them means participants need to have a completely different level of courage and persistence.

Stated bluntly, you have to eliminate the phrase "giving up" from your vocabulary.

At the end of it all, I came in 12th out of the 30 entrants – a placement that filled me with pride. Any number would have been fine. For me, it wasn't about the prize, the medal, or anything else. The internal results were always what mattered, which I knew I'd already achieved.

Above all, I was very proud of what I'd accomplished and what I had become in the process. The excitement I had was immeasurable for the endless growth opportunities I had before me. I realized something especially wonderful that day...

I had so much of myself back once again.

7

The Aftermath

So much of me was back, but there was still definitely some work to be done. In fact, it appeared that I had a new problem to overcome.

It started with a natural desire since, with all that behind me, I was ready to eat! The "no peanut butter" notes and restrictions were things of my past. I was over my family and friends saying I was too skinny, too. So, I began eating and eating and eating.

I remember being at one of my best friend's house, Kristin Padavoni. Kristin is beautiful and she resembled Marilyn Monroe with her blonde hair, sparkling eyes, and sharp features. She is so cool, calm, and collected…unlike some of us. Our whole group of friends was there, too, and I remember, I couldn't stop eating. Pretzels, ice cream, anything you could imagine. Everyone thought it was so funny.

But was it?

I found myself picturing how I looked at the competition: tan, lean, ripped. I'd never been like that before. For months and months, I'd trained hours a day, barely eating enough to survive. I'd had my body fat checked biweekly and weighed in every time, too. I'd performed cardio in a fasted state six days a week because that's what I was told to do.

I remember trying to plan the same meals as I did at first during my competition prep: grilled chicken, romaine lettuce, and flaxseed oil. By the end of the week, I was so sick of this and so hungry for all the carbs I'd been depriving myself of.

That's when I'd binge.

I know this isn't right. Why am I doing this? The competition is over.

I remember many of the other girls who worked out at the gym had some serious eating and body image issues.

I know this isn't healthy, but I can't stop.

Those days, I worked at the Big Kahuna on Fridays as a cocktail waitress. It was a great job while it lasted, and it provided a good income while I was in college. I would even get to work at all of the concerts like Lynyrd Skynyrd, John Mayer, and the Beach Boys.

Admittedly, my uniform was essentially a bikini, which wasn't my ideal. But that was the requirement.

At least they're boy-short bottoms.

That's how I rationalized it all. They triggered me anyway. I knew I had to wear the "uniform," but on Fridays, I would open up the box of plain Cheerios as a consolation prize.

This isn't so bad. They're just Cheerios.

One serving would turn into two. Then three. Then four. Then I lost count. I couldn't stop. I just kept going and going.

Just hours before I had to go to my shift, I would be so extremely full and bloated, sick, and miserable.

Why did I do that? I ate clean all week. Now I have to be in a bikini all night with my bloated belly.

Sometimes I felt so full that I'd force myself to throw up because I thought that would make me feel better. It never really did though. If I did throw up, it was so gross. If I didn't, I felt like I could crawl in a corner.

I'd tell myself I wouldn't do it again, but the same thing would happen all over the next week – mostly with Cheerios, sometimes with Triscuits or pretzels if I was being really daring. I would gain a few pounds, and then it would be gone again. I clearly wasn't as lean as I was for Miss Fitness America. I looked more lean than normal to most people.

However, I wasn't normal at all. Deep down, I knew it. I felt quite alone dealing with that deep dark secret I was keeping from even those I loved the most – yet another hurt I was bearing alone.

Then, one Sunday morning, about a year after my competition, came a day I'll never forget. I was sitting at the kitchen table with Mom sitting across the table in her curlers. She was plowing through the *News Journal* as she normally did, but she stopped to ask me if I wanted breakfast.

"No, thanks," I responded quickly. "I'm headed to the gym first."

What I didn't say was that I wanted to do my fasting cardio like I did all the time.

She looked at me with such deep concern. "Arianne, what are you doing?"

I responded defensively, as I now had a bad tendency to do. "What are you talking about?"

"This. This!" she responded, knowing both of us knew what she meant. "I'm worried about you. What's happening?"

That's when I started crying uncontrollably. The only words I could get out were, "I don't know. I don't know."

That was the moment my healing began. I didn't even tell my mom about the rape at this point. I didn't go to counseling either. Truth be told, I'm not sure it was even considered or discussed. Each day, I made huge strides in how I looked at food, exercise, and my body differently. I began to appreciate it all more and more.

I learned that there had to be a healthier way to do this. That fueled my passion for healthy nutrition and movement for everyone, not just me. Health isn't about a number on a scale, body fat percentage, or how cut your muscles are. It's about how you feel on the inside.

Truly. That sounds so cliché. But it's so much more accurate than what people realize.

It's not just physical health involved, it's emotional, mental, social, and spiritual health, too. So, in the end, I'm so grateful that my year of torment and focusing on very superficial things ended up with such intense revelations about so many things.

They helped shape me into the woman I am today.

8

An Opportunity of a Lifetime

I was finishing up my education at UD and working as a dietetic assistant at Cokesbury with my new perspective on health. Thanks to my previous experiences, I knew there was a better way. I knew that people didn't have to starve themselves or work out hours a day to stay "fit," and that they could be at peace with their bodies now that I was "on the other side" of that struggle.

At the same time, I did recognize how much mental strength I'd gained from my physical strength. Therefore, fitness and balanced nutrition remained a fundamental part of my life. When I came to this realization, I also realized that I'd been training at the wrong place. I'd learned a heck of a lot where I started, but I didn't want to focus on aesthetics anymore.

I wanted people to feel as good on the inside as they did on the outside.

A friend of mine at the Big Kahuna, Stephanie, mentioned one day that a personal training studio named L.I.F.E. was hiring. She knew the owner, Tom Starobynski, and said it could be a great place for me.

I thought she was awesome, so of course, I completely trusted her. I was guilty of that in general, but fortunately, that tendency didn't lead me astray this time.

When I got an interview there, I distinctly recall showing up in fitness clothes. You would have thought I would dress up for it; Mom had taught me better than that, for sure. But, I thought, it's a fitness studio. This should be expected.

Meeting Tom was a little intimidating. He was this muscle-built, brown-haired guy in a black muscle tee-shirt. Although, he seemed like a good guy regardless as he showed me around the studio. Small and quaint, there was equipment spread out neatly around the space. I remember seeing the deadlift rack specifically and getting emotional, thinking about how much those weights had done for me.

All around, it looked pretty intriguing, complete with a spiral staircase going upstairs. Apparently, I did a decent enough job of impressing Tom too, since he hired me on the spot, complete with the autonomy to start my own nutrition program!

I was elated, filled with ways I could help people with their fitness and nutrition, this time in a healthy way. Plus, I got to start that week, complete with two personal training clients. Tom and two other people, Doug and Eugenia, showed me the ropes; and we ended up becoming great friends, too. The clients were fantastic, especially Dave Geiger and Mark Aitken, who were always giving me life lessons as much as I was helping them.

I took it all in like a sponge.

As I implemented my nutrition programs and packages, it was so much fun to do it exactly how I wanted to. The best part was that our clients were getting results. I still had a lot to learn, I knew, but it sure was great practice and I felt like I was really finding my flow.

One day, a lady named Kim Dare came to the studio – as I was sitting on the floor eating fish that stunk up the whole studio, of course. That was a great start. She had a look in her eye like she was there for a reason.

Apparently, she already knew Tom, but there was nothing casual about her demeanor that day to indicate she'd just stopped by to say hi.

It turned out I was right about that. Kim was a physical therapist, I learned, which instantly appealed to me since, just three short years ago, that was exactly what I was planning to do with my life. She owned Physical Therapy Connection on Miller Road in Wilmington, only about 10 minutes from the studio. She was offering a space for sublease, which would make a great gym adjacent to her physical therapy practice.

The gym that was renting space from her now was moving locations. So, she was looking for another studio, and she wanted someone that met her high standards. After Tom and she talked for a bit, I sensed he was serious about this; but it wasn't until the following week that he asked if we could have a meeting.

I have to admit, I was a bit nervous. I thought I might have been in trouble. Then again, if you ask my mom, I was always so defensive back then, even if I did nothing wrong.

When we met that Wednesday afternoon, he cut right to the chase though, calming my nerves. He brought up the conversation with Kim, and when I asked him what he thought about it, he absolutely shocked me.

"I think it would be a great opportunity for us," he said. "I'd like you to be a partner."

"A what?" I genuinely thought I must have heard wrong.

"A partner."

"What are you talking about?" That probably wasn't the most savvy response ever, but it was the one I gave, and with good reason. "I haven't even graduated college yet. I still have my dietetic internship to do. I just started personal training here and getting my nutrition program off the ground. I don't even know what I would do. What does a business partner do?"

I obviously had so many questions, but he didn't.

"Relax. It will be fine." He seemed to mean it, too.

By the time we finished talking, I had calmed down a bit. Still, there was no way I could forget that I was only 21 years old. How could I be a business partner? What could I possibly bring to the table?

When I went home to mull it over, I did have to wonder what I had to lose. Besides, this could be a great opportunity – exactly what I wanted to do. This was something that would give me the chance to realize my vision for a multi-disciplinary center. It just fit so well with my vision of starting my own business someday.

That was to say nothing about how I'd be working adjacent to a very well-respected physical therapist, from whom I could learn so much from. As I had learned since she first walked into Tom's space, her academic background and professional specialty would make a great combination with my nutritional knowledge and already existent personal training skills. I knew there was so much we could do together for our future clients.

So, I went back on Thursday and told Tom I was in.

Upon officially meeting Kim – with no smelly fish involved – I shared my thoughts with her, and she agreed. When I talked to Tom about that conversation, we also came to an agreement, committing to open the business together.

The name we came up with was CORE Fitness Studio.

Admittedly, I was a bit overwhelmed as even just a 20% partner, which seemed more than enough. Riddled with excitement and nerves alike, I remember asking Kim if I could shadow her. Then, I wanted to be her patient. In all honesty, I wanted to be just like her.

Fortunately, Kim was very excited to have us, too. She helped things progress quickly, from leasing the space to signing the papers and finally getting to work. Our first few months of running CORE were quite the experience, including the innumerable hours we put in problem-solving, out-of-the-box thinking, and do-it-ourselves solutions.

The actual amount of work was outright disorienting at times.

For instance, we had a beautiful 5,000 square-foot facility, furnished with existing equipment that we leased from Kim. Yet there weren't a ton of guaranteed clients to fill it right away, so we had to hustle. We made flyers and hand-delivered them throughout the local neighborhoods around us. We designed ads for local magazines like *Out & About* and *Spark*. We learned many things along the way that led us to our grand opening.

One of the highlights for me during that period was being able to pick Kim's brain whenever we happened to be free. It was about business occasionally, but mostly it was about movement. I wanted to know everything I could about how to serve our clients better and how we could help them, which meant I had plenty of subjects to explore.

What did their injuries mean for them?

What did they mean for me?

How could I treat them properly?

I was so inquisitive, and it was so great of Kim for allowing me to be. She gave me such valuable amounts of time and feedback. Her friendship and mentorship was invaluable, for which I will always be thankful.

I'll admit I wasn't so thankful about another aspect of the business, and that would be bookkeeping. It just wasn't something I enjoyed. While it's so extraordinarily satisfying to be an entrepreneur and a small business owner, no matter how much effort one puts into it, there's still a task or two that invariably triggers groans or gasps or some other expressions of disdain. For me, like I imagine many others in my situation, keeping all the financial numbers straight simply wasn't my preferred responsibility.

Still, I had to learn it to handle the business. So, I did. Tom taught me how to manually track the client sessions and payments in handwritten detail. All the while, I was trying to give my clients the best possible care, which meant I was also looking to learn more. At the same time, I started my dietetic internship through the University of Delaware. The internship was only part-time, but still, it took up a fair amount of my availability. I would have my internship all day and then have personal training clients at night.

As per usual, I was busy, busy, busy. But I felt different about it this time around. It wasn't like before. I loved every second of it (minus the bookkeeping). I was growing and helping others to grow, too.

How amazing was that!

Life was finally feeling normal again – perhaps even better than normal – until my next big twist came along.

9

I Never Got the Chance

I couldn't wait to share with my mom how great things were going, but I never got the chance. When I called her up one Tuesday night while driving from my internship to CORE Fitness, she was crying. She was crying so hard that I knew her heart was broken.

I couldn't even understand her, her words were so muffled. She tried to get it out, "Oh, Arianne!" But her tears made it so hard to hear anything else.

I couldn't even begin to think about what could possibly be wrong. I didn't think it was my dad; they didn't even talk anymore. So maybe it was something with her health?

All I knew was it had to be something awful, scaring me so badly as I asked, "Mom, are you okay? Please tell me what happened."

Somewhere in the middle of her sobs, I heard "David."

Then I heard "cancer."

The terror only intensified. "What do you mean 'cancer'? What is going on?"

Cancer? Again? Davey has cancer? It did not compute. Could not.

Could it?

Utterly heartbroken, she replied, "Yes. It came back."

So many memories flooded in. Like how, just weeks ago, he and I were at the Stone Balloon, partying our butts off. But also how he was too sick to see me when he was at Johns Hopkins. How he was in that hospital gown.

"Mom, no!" The words ripped out of me with so much anguish.

My next flashback was of one of the stupidest things I'd ever done. One that Davey never forgot.

He was so particular about his things, especially his motorcycle and car. He would park his black Isuzu Impulse hatchback with tinted windows in the garage. Immediately to the left of that, right in the middle of the garage, he parked his sporty turquoise Suzuki motorcycle.

Well, Mom and I were out one day running some errands and, as per usual, we barely had enough room to park because of his toys, let alone bring the groceries in. As only I can do, I assessed the situation and decided I'd simply move his motorcycle out of the way. I was just going to shift it over a bit by myself to give us a few extra feet of walking room. Besides, I'd been out on the bike a few times before.

What's the worst that could happen?

I answered that question a little too well after realizing that riding on the motorcycle and moving it myself were very different things. When I grabbed the handlebars, I promptly dropped the 400-pound vehicle – which I hadn't realized was 400 pounds to begin with – right into his newly washed and waxed Impulse.

Right into it.

It was like something out of a movie. Then again, sometimes I think my life is a movie.

I immediately burst into tears like only I could do so well. It was the worst feeling in the world and inspecting the damage didn't make that go away one bit. When I finally gathered myself enough to look closer, there was no denying that the rear mirror on the motorcycle had broken off and the car was severely dented.

I couldn't believe it. How would I tell him? What will he do? As if I hadn't done enough damage to our relationship over the years just for being me, an annoying little sister. We had just started to connect at that point: to be friends.

How can I fix this?

The damage was pretty significant though. He pointed that out very quickly when he heard the chaos of me crying so hard.

I cried even harder when he showed up to the scene, trying to get the words out. "Dave, I'm sorry. I'm so sorry!"

He was furious, as I expected. "What the hell, Arianne?"

"I'm so sorry!" I sobbed some more.

That didn't calm him down. He just kept yelling for a while, and then remained fairly angry with me for about a week after that. We were living under the same roof then, so that made things awkward, to say the least. We'd pass each other in the kitchen, both reaching for the peanut butter, and he would ignore me completely.

I thought he'd never forgive me.

Then he did, as siblings are often capable of doing, despite everything. We passed each other again in the kitchen one day while I was going for my Crystal Light lemonade and he was grabbing for his iced tea. Just like that, everything seemed the same.

Davey shook his head. "You really damaged both of them at the same time."

I definitely had.

"How could you damage my two favorite things at the exact same time? Who does that?"

That would be me.

A half-smile snuck up on his face as he continued, the good-natured expression of a sibling who loves his sister through the good, bad, and ugly. "That is totally something you would do, isn't it?"

My responding smile was no doubt saturated in relief that day. This was the proof that my brother loved me unconditionally. My good-natured brother should never have had cancer even once, let alone twice.

My body felt tense all over just thinking about putting Davey and cancer in the same sentence again. I was clenching my fists, my breath was growing more shallow, and my heart was beating faster.

"Mom, no! Not again! Not again."

My eyes filled up with tears for so many reasons. This was supposed to be a thing of the past. We'd checked cancer off our family list. We already went down that emotional rollercoaster.

Just… No!

It can't be back. How could it?

Denial was overwhelming part of me. Memories were flooding back every bit as strong: how the first time, he had to go through months of aggressive chemotherapy to achieve remission, only to relapse in three months.

I didn't understand it then. I didn't understand it now.

All those years ago, after a consultation with Children's Hospital of Philadelphia (CHOP), David was referred to Johns Hopkins for a bone marrow transplant, which was considered experimental for Hodgkin's at that time. He spent Christmas at Hopkins that year, and I spent it with Grams and Pop-Pop.

He didn't come home once during that period, his schedule too full of so many treatments designed to save his life. Yet they were hell while they lasted.

When I'd finally gotten to see him, I remember being confused at the picture he presented: how humbled and weak he looked compared to his usual proud and strong self. It took some time for my six-year-old brain to compute how strong Davey really was regardless.

Because as far as I know, he never even complained. Not once. He had every reason in the world to be angry, yet he just kept pushing forward.

Dad, I know, wasn't as actively present as Mom was during Davey's treatment. He had such a hard time seeing his son like that. It was too much for him to bear.

I'm sure Mom felt the same way. Well, I know she did. She didn't let it stop her, though. She was by his side every single step. I can't even begin to imagine the pain she felt, watching her son constantly being poked and prodded at with IVs and shots. Yet she comforted him, supported him, and took care of his every need the best she possibly could.

If she could have taken the pain away from him, she would have. In a heartbeat. That's how Mom is. Always.

I realize now that it was just as hard for her to leave me back in Delaware as it was for her to watch David go through what he was going through. She probably thought she was abandoning me, but that wasn't how I saw it. I might not have been old enough to understand all of what was going on, but I knew how much she loved me.

How much she loved us.

Growing up, she would write us letters about everything, whether we were right down the road or a phone call away. That was her thing, and Davey and I, and even Dad, would get a kick out of that fact.

We also got so much out of them. I have kept so many of those letters over the years with her words of wisdom. The encouragement, support, and love she showed us are what shaped who we were and who we were meant to be. One of her favorite lines to either write or say to us was, "I love you with a passion that just won't quit."

Even when it hurt so bad.

As I sat in the car, listening to my mom cry and cry, I couldn't help but think about all she'd been through. There was nothing I could do to take this newest devastation away from her.

I was crying uncontrollably myself, but I managed to get myself together before she did. "Mom, I need you to calm down."

She didn't.

"Mom, I can't understand you," I begged. "Please. Please tell me what's going on."

She finally managed to get some words out that my brother's cancer may have returned. It wasn't confirmed yet, but it "wasn't good," as she stated.

We knew Davey hadn't been feeling well for a bit now. He had even gone to the doctor about it. But he was in remission for more than ten years. So that heartbreaking word "cancer" hadn't crossed our minds since his initial diagnosis. Yet there it was anyway: the possibility of Hodgkin's lymphoma, a cancer of the lymphatic system that's typically very curable, "they" say. Nonetheless, it's cancer.

And cancer? It sucks. Even if you've already battled it and won, it's terrifying.

I never wanted to see Davey weak again. I didn't want to see him in that hospital gown. I didn't want to see the fear in his eyes again or his devastating efforts to be strong anyway.

But, we did this before, and we would do it again.

Right?

We would have to. There was no other option. This was it. We would fight with him every step of the way.

We found out soon after that. Bucks, as we called him, had cancer, sure enough. So, Mom and I put our heads together to determine what would be best for him as he started treatment again: chemotherapy and steroids.

The steroids made him extremely puffy, which he hated so much. Fortunately, he did appear to be responding to all of it, and that was obviously the most important thing. Over time, he started feeling well enough to return to his previous habits, like barhopping with me at the University of Delaware. Then we got to hear the word we'd been striving for so hard for what felt like so long.

Cured.

The sound of those syllables put together is such a relief. It's almost indescribable to hear them spoken about someone you love too much. It felt as if a massive weight had been lifted from our family when the doctors gave us that news. Then, of course, there's a whole host of emotions that come over you, too.

He'd done it. He'd done it again.

My brother was back. This time, we were closer than ever. We looked forward to hanging out again, laughing like crazy, and him making fun of me, as per usual, which was precisely what we went on to do, loving every second of it. I have so many wonderful memories from those months.

Fenwick Island was one of my best memories, where he and I and his best friend, Brett, spent our spring break together. Looking back, it was by far the most enjoyable mid-semester escape I'd ever had. From the moment we arrived at Seacrets and the Green Turtle in Ocean City, Maryland, we were laughing together, carrying on, drinking beers, eating queso and cheese, and dancing the night away.

At one point, we got into a queso fight where we literally threw cheese all over each other. It was so fun that we eventually called that trip "Queso Island."

I felt the closest I'd ever been to my brother. He was so handsome and looked so healthy, even with his cute bald head. Too much had come about as a result of his diagnosis, including his engagement that ended somewhere between treatments. His fiancée couldn't bear the burden of it, and they eventually called it off.

That admittedly turned out to be a blessing in disguise. He had met a wonderful girl now, JoAnna, who loved him unconditionally, hairless head and all, just like we did.

JoAnna came graciously into our lives as this quiet, beautiful soul. It's hard to describe her integration into our family, but it was as if she was an angel that came down to be with him right when he needed it – to be with us, too.

I knew that Davey was really happy with her and that she meant the world to him. Furthermore, I could tell when I spoke to him that he was at ease. So, as his sister and No. 1 fan, I couldn't have been happier for him, and proud of him.

Then, the headaches started happening. They were intense, and considering Davey never complained, they had to be pretty bad. He went to get evaluated to see what was going on.

Worse yet, it was back to the oncologist.

The seizures happened before anything was determined. It was like the beginning of an end: something that prompts a point of no return.

It began on a normal night, where David was comfortably sitting on the couch with his popular sitcom airing on TV. Mom was in the kitchen, busy paying bills. I was working on my laptop, comfortably snuggled up on a reclining chair.

I'd moved back home months ago to help out with his treatments, so nothing seemed out of the ordinary at first. Yet I knew something wasn't right by the sound David started making. I didn't have to be looking directly at him when it began. They weren't normal noises, and so I looked up from what I was doing, only to see his whole body shaking out of his control.

I was at his side in the next instant. I have no idea what happened to my computer.

"Dave? Dave! Are you okay?" My high-pitched voice rose even further. "Mom! Mom! Get in here!"

My mom rushed in so fast. She must have toppled her chair in the process since I heard it clatter. Then she was at my side, trying to help me stop David's uncontrollable shaking. Even so, our combined efforts were of no use.

Mom hurried to the phone to call 911 while I kept holding him. For a moment, his shaking lessened, but only because he lost consciousness at that point.

I'm not certain which one was more frightening.

Mom and I got to ride in the ambulance with him that night. Although it was David who'd had the seizure, I'd say the EMTs would agree that all of us had the same distraught look on our faces. It had come as such a blow to all three of us, a complete surprise.

That's how I came to one of the most undesirable déjà vu moments yet again. I kept repeating in my mind that it couldn't be real. It simply couldn't have been real.

How could it be true?

The familiarity of my incredulity and fear didn't lessen their effects. Arriving at the hospital offered only so much relief. The anxious waiting time, the lingering questions and various worries were still there, as was the vain hope that it might not be as terrible as it appeared.

But it was, destined to go downhill to horrifyingly worse.

After conducting several tests on him, they finally diagnosed my brother with lung cancer. Worse yet, more tests revealed that it was the kind of aggressive lung cancer that had already metastasized to his brain.

Davey turned to me with a calm, drained resolve in his eyes after we were informed of the initial results. Then, when we went home to Mom's, he asked me to do something for him that tore me to pieces even further.

"Arianne, let's go look up lung cancer."

With or without me, I knew he was going to do it eventually anyway. It was only normal for him, the patient, to have to know. The only difference was that, if I was there with him when he was doing it, it would mean the world to him.

It's natural to want to ignore reality when a loved one is in such a tough situation: to shut it out and hold it out for as long as humanly possible. Honestly, a very large part of me wanted to remain ignorant in that position.

Yet it was never about me. So, I locked down everything inside of me that was screaming to ignore it: that it would all go away if I could only disregard the beast in the closet. I got up with him instead and we went to my room, opened my laptop, and looked up those two excruciating terms in complete contradiction to my understandable yet unreasonable feelings.

Lung cancer.

His prognosis, according to everything that came up in our searches, was not good. "Survival rate: two years," the results said. That was painful enough to read.

Then David looked right at me to put those horrific words in a full sentence: "Arianne, I have two years."

Such a very simple sentence with only five words in it. That was all. Yet in my mind, they multiplied.

Two years? That corresponds to twenty-four months. One hundred and four weeks. Seven hundred thirty days.

So much and so little at the same time.

So much because, in two years, a lot can happen. In two years, we could find a cure. In two years, a breakthrough drug might be developed, one that better matched his body and condition. Or in two years, they might be able to kill the cancer through the treatment they already intended to put him on, allowing me to enjoy more than merely 730 more days with him.

As it should have been. As I agonizingly wanted it to be.

In two years, anything could happen. Hadn't I proven it already? After all, I'd gone from knowing nothing about fitness to participating in a national fitness competition. I had gone from thinking I knew what I wanted to do in life to going after my dream career: my life's calling.

So, yes, anything is possible. Couldn't I – couldn't we – just prove it again?

The question wasn't as simple as that, of course; and no answer is as simple as that either.

After making the declaration that he only had two years to live, my brother cried and I cried with him. It was impossible not to know that I could lose him: that he thought this was it.

However, it was just as impossible for me to surrender. I just couldn't. Not with my dearest brother. Not with my family.

Feeling the same way, Mom was right there beside me so that she, my brother, and I turned into a dream team. The hospital was certainly part of the process, and it supported us along the way. I don't want to understate the medical team's role one bit, but they weren't involved in David's care the way we were. No matter what the uncertainties each day brought, the three of us battled together.

The next eight months were filled with good, and bad, and excruciating days together, but we stayed intact, nevertheless. JoAnna, who loved David then and still loves him now, remained by his side too in such a courageous manner. She was there be it a good or a bad day for him, refusing to give up on him even when he tried his hardest to push her away, no doubt for her own good.

I'm sure he didn't want her to suffer watching him deteriorate the way he did.

He started as a normal, healthy adult male who could use his arms and legs and body like most of us take for granted every day, so used to the gifts we've been given. Until he couldn't anymore. Until he lost the ability to move the whole left side of his body.

He started out being able to walk. Until he couldn't. Until he had to use a wheelchair because he was losing more and more strength. Until we reached the point where he needed our aid in transferring him from his bed to his wheelchair, even when using the bathroom.

It was horrific watching his body fall apart like that. Yet one of my best memories came from that time anyway. When I would get home, David would be there, waiting patiently for me so that I could help him with his physical therapy.

He was in his hospital bed by then, and I would sit with him and move the whole left side of his body because he couldn't. I wasn't sure exactly what I was doing at that time. Yet, I understood and loved movement and since I was watching that blessing being taken away from him, I was determined to do everything in my power to prevent that.

After those exercises were done, I would take him out in the wheelchair for a walk around the block. That was so special, too. He loved the sunshine and getting out in nature, and it was during those strolls that we had some of our best conversations. Sometimes, we wouldn't talk at all, since he might need some peace and quiet. Even then, it was just as special.

I just tried to pay attention to what he needed that day, always wondering what was going through his head. I seemed to be thinking about that all the time.

Was he scared?

Did he know he was dying?

Was he in pain?

Did he know how much we loved him?

There were some lighter moments interspersed in all of that, I'll admit; like the moment he told me in a very serious manner, "Arianne, I'm really getting concerned. Mom is getting weak. She tried to transfer me today and almost dropped me."

No matter how gloomy that statement was, I had to suppress my smile. Dave was more worried about our mother in the middle of all of this than he was about himself. That was who my brother was.

As for how strong I had to be during that time, I wouldn't have been able to do it without the help of several people, including Elaine. She was a constant friend who listened to all my worries, offered me her shoulder to cry on whenever I needed it, and shared her voice for me to listen to. She had this exceptional ability to know just what I needed and how I could be refreshed so that I could be everything my brother needed.

He needed so much, and more and more of it the longer the disease attacked him. Even so, I think we all were in some form of denial until the end of his suffering. Is it possible to get through life without some form of hope? Even just a spark?

Since he just loved Lance Armstrong, Mom and Dave would have coffee together in the morning and watch the Tour de France. With all his heart, he believed Lance was going to help find a cure.

Perhaps that can still happen. I certainly hope that it does.

My family eventually got to the point where we were all mentally and physically exhausted. David was starting to really suffer. Worse still, the disease was eating away at his organs until he could no longer talk and he needed more oxygen to breathe.

It was a Monday night, and Mom and I were sitting with him on the hospital bed, holding his hand, and telling him we loved him. Making him comfortable was the only thing we could do.

We had the radio on, and Bette Midler's "Wind Beneath My Wings" came on as we sat there. It inspired both of us to try to sing to him, though we cried the whole way through.

We'd done everything in our power to hang on to him as long as we could. Mom and I knew this was it, no matter how much we had tried to change that reality.

Whether or not David knew as he slipped away, I can't say. He went peacefully though, something I'll always be grateful for after everything he had gone through. My brother got his wings that night, October 6, 2004, shortly after the song ended.

The whole ordeal had been such a tough struggle for us all. I had missed so much of my internship and so much work and so much of everything else – none of which I regretted one bit as I sat there beside him that one last time. Being with my big brother was invaluable, and not just because of what it meant for him. That time was, is, and always will be worth it to me, too.

Besides, suddenly having my time freed up was devastating. I would have done anything possible to have my schedule all tied up again. There was just too much time to think now. To wonder why.

There was so much emotional pressure, spiritual sorrow, mental uncertainty, and even physical heaviness concentrated in that ever-present, ever-complicated, ever-sickening question of why.

Why did we have to exert so much effort to save such a precious and courageous soul, only to see the way he was taken away from us?

Why did it have to be so unfair?

Why couldn't it have been me instead of him?

Why did he always have to suffer through life, while things always seemed fine for me?

That last one might not have been exactly rational, but grief doesn't care about logic. It hits you however it hits you, and you have to navigate through it however you can.

Mom and I soldiered through those first few days, making funeral arrangements, and writing David's eulogy. It was an emotional rollercoaster, to say the least. Neither of us wanted to give that last detail to anyone else. It had to be us.

Mom was the writer in the family, of course, but I volunteered to read it. She would have been too emotional, so I thought I could handle that task. For him. It went like this:

David's first major test in adversity came at a young 11 years of age when he was diagnosed with Hodgkin's disease. He didn't want any of his classmates to know and managed to keep up with school despite his grueling chemo regimen. Fortunately, his hair only thinned, so he was able to keep his "secret."

The second blow came a short three months following his treatment when he relapsed, and we were off to Johns Hopkins for an experimental transplant. All he cared about was not missing a year of school and so begrudgingly agreed to attend the Huntington Learning Center to stay with his classmates. The years following were good years with friends, cars, girls, graduation, parties – typical teenage years.

His passion for anything mechanical shone in his love for radio-controlled cars, then go-karts, dirt bikes, and motorcycles. He was an accomplished HVAC mechanic and installed new systems for his mom, dad, grandfather, and friends.

He loved to fish, and excitedly bought new lures and re-strung his fishing rods for the opening of trout season every April with his buddies. He also enjoyed snowboarding. David held a deep fascination for weather systems, particularly tornadoes, and was a storm chaser at heart.

We thought he was home free, but again adversity struck with a relapse of Hodgkin's in 2000. He was again treated aggressively and ultimately achieved remission. At the tail end of his treatments, he met an angel, JoAnna Szczerba. He was very optimistic about life and decided to treat himself to a new truck. JoAnna was doing the financing at the Dodge dealership and, as she tells the story, when he came in, she noticed him, and when she ran his credit, etc., she thought, "Wow, he's got a house, buying a new truck, good credit, and he's cute too." They met that day… and a month later, they ran into each other… with their first date that October. She has been by his side since.

He had about nine months of freedom before a headache forced him to get checked, which ended in a diagnosis of metastatic lung cancer. This was a blow of all blows! We went back down to Johns Hopkins, but options appeared limited due to all of his prior treatments. The many procedures that followed were debilitating; however, not once did he waver in his belief that he would beat the odds. Whenever he was faced with a particularly difficult surgery or treatment, he would grow his "battle beard." He was a true warrior… with the heart of a lion!

The most devastating period for David was when he was forced on disability and then, almost a year or more later, had to relinquish his ServiceMark van because the chances were getting slimmer of his returning back to work.

All during his treatments, David pursued one project after another on his home… installing windows, working on the lawn, installing light fixtures, etc., always with the latest and greatest gadgets available and, of course, totally amazing his family and friends.

He read Lance Armstrong's book and was further inspired that he could win his race to a cure. The yellow wristbands that read LIVESTRONG have been worn by his family and friends in support of his belief. He watched Lance's fifth and sixth Tour de France "wins" faithfully.

July of 2004 was the final major blow. David had a fall and lost mobility on his left side completely. He was sent home with Delaware Hospice support and was bedfast from that time forward. Still, he never quit but utilized his physical therapist, Arianne, daily, determined to walk again, and never once complained. His one wish was to snowboard "just one more time."

There was a hummingbird feeder outside a window within a perfect view of his bed. They would entertain him, and because he knew his Mom loved them so, he would always let her know when they were feeding.

David's patience and unbelievable courage have been far-reaching. He has touched the hearts of doctors, nurses, and staff who were amazed at his unwavering tenacity, and he has been a true inspiration to everyone who knew him. He never sought special attention or sympathy. No matter who came to visit and asked him how he was doing, the response was a standard "pretty good." As his dad stated frequently, "He is one tough cookie."

Our love for him will be carried in our hearts forever, and our hope is that our brave warrior is finally at rest, free as a hummingbird, and that his heart is filled with gladness and joy for all eternity. Also that he may get a firsthand glimpse of a tornado, and his last wish at one more run of snowboarding!

I'll never forget that day. That day when I stood up at the podium speaking those words, fighting back tears every step of the way. The day we had to say goodbye to him forever.

To call it heartbreaking doesn't do it justice. I honestly don't know if there is any way to describe what we felt.

Father Greg gave the service. Although I don't remember exactly what he said, I remember thinking how perfect it was. He came to visit Davey when he was sick; and for some reason, Davey seemed to genuinely connect with him. I think it was because Father Greg was real. He didn't try to sugarcoat things. He helped him with the process of dying – if that's even possible.

When the pallbearers came to take Davey's casket out, I wanted to scream, to shriek: "Stop!" I felt like I was in a bad dream that I was going to awake from. I had to wake from it.

Yet I didn't. Everything seemed so permanent.

That November and supposedly happy holiday season were lacking joy and purpose, understandably so. If only he were there.

The purpose behind his untimely death, I just couldn't reconcile. The years that followed have not miraculously altered that. There was one thing I knew and still know: I would have gladly carried on fighting if it had meant more time with him. Mom, too.

Oh, Mom.

She was yet another big concern of mine in the twirl of emotions following David's death, posing yet another question I couldn't possibly comprehend. I didn't know what to say to her as the days went on. I had no idea how to help her resolve this immense emotional burden: this entire gaping absence of her son not being physically in her life anymore.

Plus, in a horrific twist of fate, Mom had been diagnosed with breast cancer herself while caring for him. She'll tell you it was because of stress, and I would agree.

It was like something out of a movie with the two people I loved most in the world both battling such deadly diseases at the same time. I didn't think something like that was even possible. I never knew anyone with cancer before that. The C-word was new to me and damaging, if not destroying my family, it seemed.

Mom acted as if it wasn't happening. It definitely was. I remember one time when the three of us went to Wilmington Hospital so she could have one of her many surgeries. It felt so unbelievable. There we were, my brother and I, sitting in the waiting room. I felt utterly overwhelmed with worry; about my brother beside me in a wheelchair with minimal function in his one arm and leg and about my mom lying still on a hospital table being cut open.

How could this be?

She carried on with the most unbelievable grace though. She was so strong, focusing completely on David's pain instead of herself. That was her sole purpose, and even her own cancer wasn't going to get in the way of that.

I'm not sure anyone could completely comprehend this unless they saw it with their own two eyes, which I did. I watched it, day in and day out, as she gave everything she possibly had to care for my brother.

Part of me even felt guilty that I wasn't giving her as much attention. Should I be? Was she dying in front of me every bit as much as he was?

I think deep down, I must have had faith that she would be okay. Perhaps it was either that or just lose it altogether.

Fortunately, Mom's cancer went into remission by the end of the first year after David died – and after about seven operations that were mainly attributable to complications from a prior operation. She's been cancer-free since then, for which we are very thankful.

Yet I couldn't help but understand, in the middle of all that and even thereafter, how all she'd ever really wanted for David was for him to survive. I got that on a very personal and intimate level. She just wanted him to live happily and to experience life just like any other young person should. So how much consolation was surviving when he hadn't?

How can I make her feel better about losing a child? What words could possibly exist?

Of course, there were none. I knew it. That didn't mean I wasn't desperate enough to want to find some magical, feel-better word.

Then the questions for myself came up. I had lost a brother, after all. A confidant. Someone who, for so long, had been my purpose. What did I do from there? What was I supposed to do without him?

What can I do?

For a time, I wasn't really sure who I was. I just couldn't see my way to anything worthwhile through the clouds of sorrow that hung around me everywhere I looked. I was totally lost.

Getting lost like that isn't just terrifying. It's bewildering, stressful, and discouraging – an engulfing tsunami of life-changing unhappiness. In that situation, people just want someone to tell them how to get over it: "Take this and call me in the morning if for some reason it doesn't work."

Yet no one has the magic pill you can take to get rid of it.

That's how, under an onslaught of that depression, I found myself asking Davey for help. I even said it out loud in a state of desperation. I couldn't do this on my own. I wanted – needed! – my big brother to tell me how to deal with not having my big brother with me anymore.

"Dave, What do I do?" I asked. "Please help me."

As I heard myself say those words, they squeezed through my ears, through the pain, and through my mind, leaving me struck deeply by the answer. It was a real answer, too. Two of them, in fact, even if they came in the form of two more questions.

But this time, they were rather encouraging ones, and I knew I had to give a voice to them.

"What would Dave want me to do? And how can I make him proud?"

It was in that instant when the haze started to fade slowly, and the road before me began to become visible again. I could honor Dave's memory best by supporting people and changing their lives for the better.

That would be my purpose.

That would be the thing that drove me.

Better yet, I know beyond a shadow of a doubt that Dave would have approved if he heard how that one-way conversation had influenced my life's purpose.

10

Purpose

Ultimately, I got to pursue that life's purpose in a way I couldn't have predicted. Moreover, it was in a way that left me scared, depressed, and incredibly angry all at the same time; since I became the sole owner of CORE Fitness within just days of my brother's passing.

Even thinking about it now, it's all kind of a blur.

It had come to light in the middle of everything that Tom and I had somewhat contradictory philosophical differences. It wasn't enough to make us hate each other, but it was intense enough that we realized we weren't bound to work together in a gym. We just could not find a reasonable common ground we could both feel good about, so we ended up wishing each other well and parting ways.

He wasn't in the best place at the time when he gave me the option to take over the business completely. Obviously, neither was I when I said yes. At first, I felt like I'd gotten the raw end of the deal, literally left with no money in the account. I was starting from ground zero, at the very moment when my whole life was turned upside down.

Yet it was CORE Fitness Studio that allowed me the opportunity to realize my new goals. That small personal training studio in Wilmington, Delaware, opened the doors for me to finally fulfill the promise I had made to my brother.

After I got through my fear, depression, and anger over my business situation, I remembered what Davey had given me. Purpose. I also reminded myself just how much I loved CORE Fitness. Put together, this was the opportunity of a lifetime.

Running the studio as a one-woman operation, I'll admit, was a stumbling block I never expected. I remained steadfast and committed to my promise to David and to myself, realizing as the weeks and months went on that I was truly excited to be on my own. Finally, I had the freedom to run things the way I wanted them to be run.

That opportunity opened so many doors, allowing me to meet wonderful people whose stories and capabilities were amazing, too – everyone from the staff I hired to the clients we signed on. The entire experience taught me so much about human movement and proper nutrition, helping me pass on life-changing information to those who needed it the most.

Put simply, it allowed me to discover my full potential.

I grew my experience in health, nutrition, and fitness with people from all walks and stages of life. That fueled my desire to be the best in the industry. At CORE, for example, I would conduct sessions for people who were just starting to delve into the fitness world or help others recover from injuries. At the same time, I would devote time to top athletes whose physical conditions were already at their peak, showing them how to better prepare for their upcoming shows, competitions, physical testing, pageants, and even the Olympics.

It was amazing!

Many of the clients I took on came to be family to me, like Barb Blumberg, Lisa Lekawa, and Carol Thomas. They were some of my favorite ladies that took care of me, just as much as I took care of them.

My staff and I had such special bonds with our clients: as we listened to their stories, challenged them to challenge themselves, and celebrated with them whenever they successfully overcame their obstacles.

CORE also became deeply involved in the community because of my passion to "pay it forward." We supported charities by hosting Thanksgiving food drives, shoe drives, and food drives for the Sunday Breakfast Mission, even adopting a family every year. We participated in plenty of 5Ks for cancer research and I initiated an annual event called DanceSTRONG a couple of years after David passed away.

As the name implies, DanceSTRONG shares the joy of dancing while raising money for cancer, showcasing various inspiring dance routines with the goal of bringing the community together for a greater cause. All proceeds go to the Livestrong Foundation in honor of Dave, and it continues to hold a special place in my heart to this day.

There was also the annual holiday party we hosted, which I will never forget, in that first business of mine. For 13 years, we celebrated health, happiness, and friendship together every December, making sure it was special for everyone who attended. There was always a human pyramid to look forward to, for one thing, comprised of people like the Marshall twins: Adam Marshall, a CORE Fitness trainer; and his inseparable brother, David, also known as Diamond Dave.

Clients and my family and best friends would come too, in large part to see that feat. Another wonderful memory for me was singing karaoke with my dad, particularly to "White Christmas" by the Drifters.

That was easily my favorite night of the year.

There were plenty of great nights and days there, though. I had the best crew that I could always depend on. I was one proud employer, to say the least, especially every time I saw them train and teach their clients with passion and enthusiasm. I know it's a cliché to say we were more like family than business associates, considering how so many companies lay claim to that concept. We literally lived it out together every workday, supporting each other just as much as we were there for our clients.

Stacy, Dave, Ashley, Jenn, Jess, Adam, and James were just some of my "CORE crew." They brought so much joy to my work and my life, and I looked forward to coming in each day because of them. We shared countless laughs and wonderful memories along the way.

Throughout all that, I was gaining valuable experience, making me more and more certain of what I still hold true today: that enhancing and extending our movements enables us to do the things we want to do. It's so much bigger than that. For the reason that, as we're able to push ourselves appropriately, our entire bodies respond better, as do our minds and souls.

Talk about winning – not just a couple of times, but threefold!

Between that discovery and the sincere desire of CORE to make a significant lasting difference in our clients' lives, I continued to gain more knowledge about the human body. There was always something new to learn – always something bigger and better to explore, and therefore no end to this extraordinary, self-appointed quest. This drove me to improve my own skills in a professional and personal context as well.

One of the ways I did that was, whenever I had a client, I would learn what he or she did for a living and what activities or sports they participated in. Let's say one would specialize in tennis, in which case, I'd take tennis lessons the next week to understand what it involved. At another point, I had a group of golfers, so I started collaborating with golf pros, opening up even more business connections and possibilities along the way.

I established the CORE Fitness methodology alongside all this, or perhaps because of it, to make sure that my team continually provided our client's performance training that carried the highest possible quality. This was focused on comprehensive continuing education, which I further carried out by shadowing Kim and personally researching existing training techniques to support the theories I developed as a result.

Before I knew it, I didn't just have a system on my hands. I had a mantra: a commitment designed to teach my team the significance of their role in the lives of others. Seeing how much influence they had and could have was what I wanted for them.

With that in mind, my methodology training covered areas such as posture, movement assessments, stability and mobility training, corrective exercises, performance training, recovery, sleep, nutrition, and so much more. As it was totally impossible to expect them to absorb everything in one go, we made it a practice to meet weekly to discuss the important matters and the ways to improve implementation.

That way, clients were always progressing at varying levels on their fitness journey, be it a week, a month, or a year since they'd first begun. Each of them had their own stories and situations that they shared with me, along with their disappointments, setbacks, and sufferings. At the beginning of their treatments, I could see and feel their frustrations for not being able to complete their dreams and goals.

It might be a woman who had wanted to play a certain sport but couldn't due to physical limitations, or a man who was counting down the days to a long-awaited vacation with his family but was worried about his inability to keep up with them. Other times, it would be a simple, every-day desire that was no less meaningful: perhaps the mere desire to play with their children without being tired and short of breath.

Lack of proper dexterity has a way of affecting people in so many ways, both inside and out.

The thing is, the majority of us have a bad habit of taking things for granted. Somehow, in a corner of our minds, we believe we'll always be able to move and bend, twist and turn, the way we always have. It really isn't an intellectual understanding, since we understand on a logical level that we're going to get older. It is hard to think that far down the road, especially when limited mobility comes sooner rather than later, because of an accident or compromised function.

Or cancer.

I saw it with my brother as the disease literally ate away at him, depriving him of all the physical abilities he once enjoyed. In no time at all, that kind of burden on the body can lead to emotional and psychological repercussions. I saw it in my brother far before I fully recognized it in my patients.

Working with him to move his arms and legs when he no longer could gave me an up-close-and-personal experience in seeing how those movements made him feel better, emotionally and physically. He looked forward to those sessions; they were a positive part of his day that not only affected his muscles and nerves but also his mood, clarity of mind, and very sense of being.

In return, that marked improvement was his gift to me despite not being the kind that could cure his cancer.

Helping others in that way was part of my healing process over his loss. I also realized at some point that I should put that same power to practice in my own life. I deserved and needed a focused personal growth challenge just as much as the people I worked with.

That's why I decided to take on another movement challenge. This time around, it was Miss Delaware USA.

My underlying rationale was that the winner got a full scholarship to pursue an advanced degree at the University of Delaware. In which case, I could use it toward the school's doctor of physical therapy program.

However, that wasn't the only thing driving me to join the pageant. The training involved also appealed to me. In order to put my best competitive foot forward against all those other strong and accomplished women, I would have to overcome a set of specific challenges, such as interviewing, fitness and nutrition training, and learning to walk on stage in heels, of course.

The bonus consideration was how it would give me a whole new voice for encouraging health and wellness in the community, starting with my fellow competitors. The overall thinking among such young ladies, of course, is that skinny is good: That as long as they can make themselves look attractive in the process, they had a good shot of taking the title.

Essentially, they think that the thinnest girl will win, a belief the judges and audience don't always dissuade them from.

If I shared space behind the scenes with them though, I could go through what they were going through with the chance to speak to them one on one and perhaps influence their thinking. If everything went exceptionally well, I could even foster a healthier outlook in the pageant culture in general.

I did everything I could to prepare for Miss Delaware USA, determined to do my absolute best. Not only did I want to look good in this newest physical fitness competition, but I also wanted to feel good on the inside, too.

This was a second opportunity to do it my way – a healthy way.

It's easy to look skinny, in my opinion. I could have simply cut a lot of certain calories, done a lot of cardio, and called it a day. Though, it takes hard work and dedication to be truly fit. That was my message to my clients, and I wanted to practice what I preached.

So, I trained hard. I lifted heavy – appropriate – amounts of weight, did regular cardiovascular activity, ate extremely healthy and clean, and made sure to prioritize sleep and recovery. All the while, I was creating a slight calorie deficit, which meant my protein needs were higher.

I learned a lot during that time. My mother always tells me that's how most worthwhile experiences are meant to be. The longer I live, the more I realize how right she is.

This did happen so quickly after Dave passed away, making me question more than once how I could possibly move forward with it. Everything seemed so superficial to me at the time. How could I be worried about my dress, my hair, my makeup, and my interview outfit considering such a huge loss?

If my brother taught me anything, it was to never give up. I've never forgotten that lesson, and it didn't fail then either.

Besides, I knew he was there in spirit, which made an enormous difference.

The love I received from my support system was unforgettable. I'll never forget Jennifer Behm, in particular. She was my interview coach and so much more: a beautiful, blonde fashionista with curly hair, who deserves her own special mention. She was a fantastic mentor, who gave me great tips and skills that I could use for a lifetime.

She also taught me how to walk on stage in four-inch heels. You have no idea how much I practiced walking. The reason why I didn't ultimately trip and fall flat on my face was because she showed me all the moves.

When I arrived for the pageant weekend, I was paired up with my roommate, Cara. I felt so lucky to be with a seasoned pageant girl with an awesome personality to boot. I felt empowered and energized all around, which was good, considering how the weekend was jam-packed with rehearsals and choreography, group numbers, and getting to know some of the other beautiful ladies.

Then it was finally time. All of the preparation leading up to this day was finally over, and now it was time to shine. It was an unbelievable feeling that day. Sure, I was extremely nervous, but I had given it my absolute all to be my best, and it showed. I'd spent months getting sponsors to help me with my dress, interview preparation, and advertisements in the pageant book. I was doing an internship with Brandywine School District, at that point, and they were so kind to sponsor me, as well as so many others.

I tamped down my fears, thought of Dave, and walked out onto that stage to proudly and confidently look out at the judges, audience, and all my friends and family who had come to support me.

There were Allison and her mom and dad, who were holding up signs for "World Peace" that couldn't help but make me smile. JoAnna was there, as well as David's best friend, Brett. My beloved cousins, Teesie and Trish; Kim, my parents… I wanted to cry when I looked out to see each of them in the much larger crowd, giving me their endless support and encouragement.

No doubt, that's what helped me make it to the final round, and up against several impressive competitors, too. My heart was racing from the shock, my breath was a bit more shallow, and I was filled with this overwhelming sense of gratitude.

Pride, too, I'm not ashamed to say. The pride I felt while standing there was unfathomable, regardless of what the outcome would be. I was standing there after months of preparation while simultaneously running a business, caring for my brother, completing my dietetic internship, and getting ready for my registered dietitian licensure exam, a commitment I made before Dave was in hospice.

I'd done my best to keep it, and I was still on track despite everything.

As I relished every second of that moment, Susan, the master of ceremony, announced we would "now be heading into the final questions phase." Or something like that. Don't expect me to remember exactly what her words were. I wasn't even quite sure what they were at the time they were going on, though I do vaguely recall her saying something like, "We'll have each contestant come up and pick her question from the fishbowl."

I was the fifth in line for that phase, which meant I got to watch four other young women walk across the stage, approach the fishbowl, and hand their pieces of paper to Susan. Then, each one in turn gave their answers as nicely, clearly, and impressively as possible.

I'm certain they all sounded and looked gorgeous as they did. Perhaps I should have been paying more attention to them. However, at that point, I was too deep in my own mind to pay attention to anything but my looming question, whatever it might be.

My brain fixated especially on what I had written on my delegate's profile, transforming each answer I'd given back into the question it had started out as.

"Arianne, what words would you use to describe society?" I could imagine Susan asking.

In which case, I would answer, "Diverse, nurturing, and evolving. Thank you."

Or "How would you define beauty?"

I would answer, "It is not the world's perception of outer beauty, rather it is a person's inner beauty, revealing character and goodness that does not fade over time."

Those were just some of the many possible questions I'd gone through before it was my turn to hear the real one intended for me.

"Arianne, please come up for your final question," Susan instructed.

And so, I did, picking from the fishbowl.

"How would you describe society as industrialized?" she asked.

After all the mental rehearsals I'd done mere moments and even seconds ago, that threw me off. It did not compute, leaving me blinking in total and utter confusion. Hence the reason why the words, "That wasn't my word to describe society," came out of my mouth.

As such, it was Susan's turn to blink in bewilderment. "I didn't say it had to be your question."

I heard the clarification, but I didn't know what to do about it. I'm certain I must have said something else to her because, after a long pause, she collected her thoughts and put us back on track.

"Would you like to pick another question from the fishbowl?"

"Yes. I would."

I did, this time selecting another something – something that wasn't about the industrialization of society. I'm certain of that, at least. All else from that little piece of paper has been lost in the haze of time since.

None of it mattered, however. Not then, not now. Not when one part of my mind was so confident. At the end of the day, the question was meaningless because I already knew my answer.

I had always known my answer.

Standing there, the entirety of reality dawned on me, along with an appreciation of where I was in the world. I was situated on a stage with a lot of people looking at me to see if I was beautiful and poised and smart, and to judge me in all categories possible. However, that spotlight turned out to be my saving grace on this occasion and in so many others.

In moments like that one, I always seek the support of the most important people in my life, including Dave. He had never once let me down, so I went straight to him for the strength and inspiration I needed, finishing my answer to Susan and the crowd in front of me with, "I'm going to live my life in honor of my brother."

At the end of the segment, all of us contestants were instructed to leave the stage, which gave me another sense of absolute understanding. Dressed up in my strapless, A-line, cherry-red gown with my makeup so skillfully done and my fellow contenders equally dressed around me – all vying for a title – I once again realized that my purpose was much greater.

In the end, it didn't matter if I won or lost. What really mattered was how I played the game.

A cliché? Sure. But once again, it was no less true.

As expected from the final phase of the pageant, I didn't win. I didn't mind that much at that point, however. As soon as I was allowed off stage, I made my way to my supportive friends and family, ready to smile and laugh at the experience. Kim was swift to joke about how I was "the only one with the muscles on that stage!" We all laughed for months – actually years – about my response: "I didn't pick that word to describe society."

Even if I had won though, I wouldn't have celebrated for long. It would just have been another challenge for me since what always matters is the process. What I've learned so far in life and continue to learn is that there's nothing like discovering and enjoying every single journey we're on; that and welcoming new opportunities to move forward and upward.

Even when they're hard.

11

Loss

After months of applying and training for the Miss Delaware pageant, the loss of Davey certainly started to set in. As Mom and I were trying to navigate the grieving process, there were so many more moments filled with the quiet certainty of loss. For one thing, it seemed as though our holiday dinners got smaller and smaller. I remember my mom and I eating Thanksgiving dinner together, reminiscing about all the people who would sit at the table with us.

We were still so heartbroken and trying to find our way. Because I didn't know what to say to Mom, we both seemed to be living in the same house yet grieving on our own. My dad, meanwhile, definitely couldn't deal with what was happening; so, unfortunately, that meant he didn't know what to say to me either. He turned to what he knew best: alcohol.

Sadly, we didn't speak for almost a year afterward.

At the time, I just didn't understand that distance. Even years later, it's still hard to comprehend despite how much more I've learned about addiction.

There were so many miserable milestones we had to get through that year. Our dog, Rocky, stuck around as long as he could to be with Davey.

He was so sick and declining fast, but my brother loved him so much. So, we prayed that he would hold out as long as possible, which he did.

When we had to put him to sleep shortly after, the veterinarian said, "Don't worry. This will be peaceful."

I wish that had been true, but that wasn't the case. The injections didn't work, drawing out the process so much longer than it should have been. It was a horrifying experience, as he seemed to just not want to go.

I felt like I hadn't been prepared for death yet was forced into a crash course on it. It's not something we understand or even talk about in our culture. Yet there I was, learning all too fast.

Shortly after, Pop-Pop, my mom's dad, passed away suddenly from a heart attack. Worse yet, he wasn't found until a day later. Tragedy on top of tragedy on top of tragedy.

Pop-Pop, the "Chief," was one of a kind. He was always tough on the outside but deep down had a heart of gold.

Years before that, one of Mom's good friends from high school, "Reds," sought her out. Mr. Wortman, as I knew him, was a kind man with red hair and classic pale skin with freckles. Although Davey had a bit of a hard time with Mom dating again after the divorce, I thought it was great.

I saw her face light up when she saw him, and they had so much fun together. They would go out dancing and talk for hours. It was almost as if they were soul mates. He was so sincere and loved us all very much, making it easy to become close to the whole Wortman family – Tara, Dana, Randy, Charles, and Coty.

Yet Mr. Wortman was diagnosed with non-Hodgkin's lymphoma as my brother was going through treatment. It's a cancer that starts in the white blood cells called *lymphocytes*, which are part of the body's immune system.

If that news wasn't devasting enough, there was also a tumor on his spine. Worse yet, when they performed radiation, it paralyzed him from the waist down.

I watched my mom take care of him after that for four years. She figured out how to manage the wheelchair, and they still went out on the town. After my brother's passing, I watched her struggle more and more. Not necessarily physically, like Davey had thought, but mentally. Emotionally.

It was all too much.

Toward the end, when Mr. Wortman was under hospice care, Mom and I were taking turns going over to his house to help with things. He was confined to the hospital bed, but I used to love chatting with him anyway. He truly had a heart of gold, and I knew he was so worried about Mom.

I was worried about her, too. I didn't think she could take much more.

Truly, I didn't feel like I could either.

Apparently, we had to, once again watching a loved one's gift of movement being taken away. Watching him fight for his life. Watching him slip away anyway, just like with my brother.

When Mr. Wortman passed in July 2006, right on the heels of Pop-Pop, I think we had a sense of relief despite the heartbreak. The kind of toll that experience takes is enormous. While Mom would have never admitted it, I knew she needed rest.

What rest could be found, since my dear Grams was next, a few months later? The woman who took care of me all those years ago, who took me on adventures to the city of Wilmington, who bought me my doll clothes, who spoiled me to no end: She was gone. We think it was cancer, too, as she'd been having significant digestive issues for some time and lost a considerable amount of weight.

As a larger woman, she always said, "If I start losing weight, you'll know something is wrong." And I guess that was true.

I'll never forget my grandmom's funeral. I was so heartbroken, but I thought I could deliver her eulogy anyway – just like I did for Davey. I stood up there at the church altar and looked out at all our family while I began to read what I'd written.

It didn't take me long before I simply fell apart.

I broke down crying hysterically. Uncontrollably. Although I don't remember exactly what happened, my mom told me that JoAnna came to the rescue. I genuinely do believe she was put into our lives for a reason.

Why do we not appreciate the ability to move until it's taken away?

Why is it that some people throw their lives away, while others are fighting to save theirs?

There were so many questions I continued to ask myself about death. Perhaps there were no easy answers to be had. That didn't mean answers didn't exist.

All that while, I was learning more and more about death. About grieving. About life. And about movement, for better and for worse.

12

Dancing After David

ork was such a bright spot for me in the middle of all of that, considering how I loved what I was doing so much. I found myself so inspired and challenged when I was able to coach someone. In fact, it was one of the things that motivated me the most.

I felt truly blessed for each opportunity that came my way in this regard. I still do today.

I love learning about people and building relationships. Not only simply discussing their fitness and health goals, but embracing the challenge of meeting them where they are and getting them where they want to be. The way they thank me throughout the process is just as wonderful, no matter whether we achieve things through small steps or big steps.

They're not the only ones who benefited, because I may have learned even more from them. They have taught and inspired me, too, over the years. Them trusting me with their very aspirations and goals gave me purpose and meaning to work my way through my own difficulties.

It feeds my soul.

With that said, I may have loved it a little too much. With my all-in personality, I tend to let things like that overtake me, getting so wrapped up in what I love that I often fail to remember how there might be other endearing sights, sounds, and experiences to dive into in this huge wide world of ours.

I prefer to give my whole self to everything that I do, which absolutely has its upsides. However, that can be at the cost of other things, whether it's personal relationships, finances, self-care or, the biggie, organization and cleanliness. It was lucky for me that I'd share with clients every bit as much as they shared with me: the nice, the bad, and the funny stuff alike. We got to know each other well that way.

This eventually led Gynnie, one of my regulars, to admitting something to me one day. "Arianne, I'm worried about you. You're working too much."

At that instant, she sounded very much like my mom. As such, I already had a response that was reassuring, guaranteeing her that I loved what I did and that I was happy with my life the way it was. It was just a year after Davey passed away and although I wasn't doing what the typical 23-year-old was doing, I believed that I was right where I should have been.

She wasn't completely convinced though. "That's wonderful, and I'm so happy for you. But if you don't develop some other interests, that happiness isn't going to last very long."

That made me pause – until she offered the most delightfully ridiculous follow-up suggestion: that I take dance lessons.

I swear I laughed about that one for almost a full minute before I was able to tell her that dancing wasn't something I did very well. Shoot a jump shot, sure. And bring on the deadlifts. But dancing?

Not so much.

However, Gynnie was quite determined. She wasn't up for "no" as an answer. "It's really fun, and the movements you'll learn are really challenging."

Movement? Challenge?

She was officially speaking my language. Now that my curiosity had been ignited, I inquired if she had a good suggestion about a great starting point.

"Starliters Dance Studio." That's what she said, and the way she described the place was really attention-grabbing. It apparently had a great instructor, a nice group of dancers, it offered group classes at least twice a week, and it was just right down the road.

Within that week, I booked my first appointment for a salsa class. I know it's not the easiest dance for a beginner, most especially for someone known for the "mom dance." That's just how I do things, for better or worse, though.

I also convinced my mom to come along with me. Actually, I coerced her. The ultimate result – that she was there with me – was the same.

The next Thursday, I brought my poor, nervous mother through the doors of the church the group was meeting at. I may have been a little nervous myself, but that started to fade away right at the entrance, where two of the most welcoming faces greeted us. Fay and Bernadette, as they introduced themselves, both looked so stunning and classy, from their gorgeous gray hair to their long, flowing skirts.

They seemed like seriously seasoned dancers to me, but they weren't uptight about their skills at all. After they welcomed us warmly and checked us in, I expressed how excited I was about the night. Their response was a great combination of undervaluing irony and good humor.

"For what?"

I could tell right away that I was going to love these ladies.

For Mom, though, she was not enjoying the experience as much. The nerves were still strong with her.

Even before the class officially started, at least 80 people were already there, smiling and happy and ready to try out their moves. Several were already out onto the floor practicing. They all looked like they were having fun, although I didn't have the slightest idea about what dances they were performing.

It wasn't that long before the instructor, Brian Wells, came to present himself. He was quite friendly and very professional, with that unique presence many dancers have: a blend of style and grace. At that moment, he made me feel like I was certainly in the right place, from his personality to the dance moves he began to demonstrate.

The class began, and my poor mom couldn't have been more intimidated. While there I was, getting more excited as Brian explained how he would teach the class. He would teach the ladies' part, then the mens', then later pair us together.

So we started.

Fortunately, nervous or not, Mom had more than a few good-natured giggles with me as we tried to follow along. We weren't familiar with the dance terminology, but we tried our best. On our own, it was hard enough, I'll admit. It became even more so when we were paired up.

I found myself laughing and laughing in between apologies as we rotated from one guy to the next. All I could say was, "Oh, sorry. Sorry again!" as I literally misstepped left and right. This included instances where I "misstepped" on my dance partners' feet, for which they consistently remained gracious.

I realized I hadn't laughed so much in a very long time; not since before my brother passed. I only became conscious of it when the class was finally over.

The experience hadn't just been invigorating and uplifting; it was also encouraging. At least, it was for me. Mom also laughed harder than she had in a long, long time. Though she made it known, all the same: that was it for her.

She'd bravely conquered one lesson. She'd conquered that hurdle. There was no need for her to go back.

As for me, I wasn't going to lie and convince myself I hadn't been terrible out there on the dance floor. It didn't matter. I was hooked. So, I signed up for the next five-week salsa course I could take, already laughing and apologizing to whatever gentlemen would be in the class as I did.

They would probably need to either avoid me, or buy sturdier shoes.

The paid class was just as good as that free one. Actually, it was even better, and I learned so much! Not long after it finished, Starliters arranged a dance social that I didn't hesitate to attend.

I was so thrilled! I couldn't wait to demonstrate all the things I'd been taught.

For the record, Mom was very happy for me after I told her about the event. She said she hoped I had a wonderful time and mentioned how she would enjoy it as well – just away from the dance floor, sitting on the sidelines.

I got right to planning my first post-course dance outfit. It was a big deal, in typical female fashion, and I even put my hair up in something besides my usual ponytail. What more did I need?

Looking back, I realized I might have looked like a football player with that particular black dress I chose. It was my usual struggle: fitness clothes or dance clothes. I found it cute at the time, and that was what mattered.

Now, I figured I wouldn't be the very best dancer in the world after just one five-week lesson. When I arrived, however, whew! Were there some pros or what? Everyone moved around the floor so gracefully in so many different kinds of dances. While I truly enjoyed seeing them show off their talents, I had to wonder when they were going to play salsa.

This question led to another question, however. If they were playing salsa, then what was I supposed to do? Could I ask somebody to dance? Did they ask me?

What was the appropriate protocol here?

The last formal dance I went to was when I was at Salesianum; when I was in high school. That dynamic was a whole lot different, I could tell. There should, naturally, be some clear variations between a dance intended for teens and one meant for mature adults, one should presume. As I did.

Which meant I was stepping into foreign waters.

As I stood on the sidelines, hoping for someone to pick me up, this sweet older gentleman named Earl came over to ask if I wanted to do the jitterbug. On his end, it was a kind gesture, but I had to be truthful and confess that I had no clue how to go about it.

Nevertheless, "I will teach you," he proclaimed. With that, we headed over to the dance floor.

It started with Earl attempting to educate me on the jitterbug ropes. Then one person after another was offering to teach me something else after that. They were all wonderful teachers, no matter how well – or terrible – their students did.

Once again, I undeniably laughed a lot during the night. Likewise, I stepped on a significant number of feet. "Sorry!" was my evening expression, to the point where I found myself pondering repeatedly, *Dear God, why do they keep asking me to try something new? I might just kill someone with these moves!*

There was a group dance lesson at some point that somehow spared my life and many feet. I figured it had to be an indication that I needed guidance, in which case, it was a sign I wasn't going to fight.

After practicing some fundamental foxtrot moves, I was right back out there for the free-for-all again before the night concluded. I had sweat streaming down my face by then, my hair was unkempt, and my belly hurt so bad from laughing. All I could wonder about was wearing the heck out of my "I survived my first social dance" T-shirt from then on.

Despite having so much fun that evening, I got a clear memo about how much I still had to learn. It was good, on the one hand, to accept this very obvious fact. On the other hand, I just wanted to be better. To express myself outside of work like that felt like such a great opportunity for me: something that felt like private recreation, yet still challenging.

Considerably challenging.

That's why I ended up signing for private lessons with Brian. Of course I did.

From the get-go, Brian asked what he usually asks his clients: "What are your goals? What do you want to get out of this?"

They were interesting questions, but I had my answers already and they all centered around movement. How much I enjoyed the challenges it presented. How much I craved it. That's why I urged him not to ease up on me. I was ready to handle whatever he could throw at me.

He took me at my word without putting too much pressure on me either. That's just the kind of teacher he was, a very good one. He clearly knew when to back off and let me process new information and precisely when to push me – the perfect form of education. It was so clear that it wasn't just a job for him. It was a passion.

Thanks to him and a lot of practice, I began to feel that I was getting quite good at this whole dancing thing. I wasn't the only one who came to that conclusion considering how Brian eventually asked me to perform with him at fundraising events.

I'm glad to say; I dared to take him up on that offer.

I have to admit that my confidence waned when it was actually go-time that first event we paired up at. Our first appearance was at a benefit for breast cancer, a matter that was too close and personal for me to even think about laughing off any mistakes I might make.

In the hours before we took the stage, what had begun as the prospects for such an exciting adventure grew increasingly more daunting to contemplate.

I understood that the ultimate purpose of the fundraiser wasn't about me showing off my skills. It was to support people coping with breast cancer. Nevertheless, I was so anxious for my own sake, for the people who paid money to see a show of art, and for Brian, who had worked so hard to teach me.

I just wanted to do well.

We had prepared for so long. But what if it wasn't enough on my part? What if I forgot the steps? What if I wasn't ready?

Ready or not, our prompt came anyway. Walking out into the middle of the floor, Brian and I took up our positions to wait for the first haunting notes of Celine Dion's "I'm Alive" to flow through the speakers. As it did, we started our dance.

The anxiety didn't instantly dissipate, but the preparation did kick in. My body understood what to do, and so did my spirit. Even better, with every new step, I could feel my brother encouraging me more. I could feel the struggles of those people there battling cancer, such powerful factors that drove my movements to flow as they should.

I may have made a few small mistakes during the whole dance, but they were nothing like my beauty pageant blooper. Yet there was a major similarity in the end result. I had a very clear realization even before the last chord faded away that, behind this newest movement challenge, I had found meaning.

It was another affirmation that I was right where I needed to be, and I realized I wanted to do more of it. More dancing. More uplifting. So much more.

I intended to use this newfound mission to help as many individuals as I could, a goal that Brian himself understood so well. He was more than happy to follow that path with me after I shared it with him. We ended up spending several years practicing new dance moves and routines, performing at fundraisers throughout the community, and supporting as many individuals as we could in the process.

As with CORE Fitness, there was a huge personal benefit in those efforts. The further I explored the dance world, the more I understood how much more there was to learn and understand! It stimulated my mental skills together with my emotional and physical ones, opening up doors to explore new wisdom from top industry leaders through books and continuing education courses. That self-motivated study paid off, often through "eureka" moments that felt as if I was taking revolutionary leaps forward.

What the human body is and what it is capable of doing is simply phenomenal.

Though, admittedly, so is its ability to feel pain. That was becoming more and more clear as well.

13

New Realization

*T*his latest stage of awareness prompted me to ponder a new realization: that I wasn't nearly as competent as I wanted to be in addressing physical distress. In which case, there was only one ultimate answer to my question of how I could improve.

Officially, I had met my next challenge.

This time around, it was to pursue an advanced education degree within the healthcare industry: physical therapy, specifically. It seemed that my original educational priorities hadn't been completely off-kilter after all. I may not have realized it all along, but I had been following a similar road with it for years.

Physical therapy is such an amazing profession, with so much to teach and offer. The more I engaged myself in it, the more I knew that my first academic love was deeply rewarding, providing individuals the chance to reduce their pain in creative and inspiring ways.

Easy remedies like drugs, medications, and pills can fail far too quickly. Plus, they come with health consequences on our bodies, our thoughts, our attitudes, and even our ability to do whatever we're medicating up for in the first place. I learned this by watching my brother and also my clients day in and day out. Generally speaking, they aren't a solution and should only be taken after thorough and careful consideration.

Physical therapy, however, evaluates and addresses the root of the problem. It then manages it from there. It doesn't mask anything, making it a much more efficient, balanced, healthy, and holistic solution. The fact that it helps me develop deeper, more trust-based relationships with my clients that can last a lifetime isn't anything I'm going to object to either.

I really didn't know how hard it would be to get a doctorate in this area right away. That's what research is for: to get you prepared to tackle what you want to try out. Before I left the consideration stage of the process, I got a hint and then some, leaving me with a pretty good idea of what I was getting into by the time I dedicated myself to it.

It was an incredibly thrilling and intimidating decision at the time. Thrilling because the more I read and saw and heard about it, the more I realized this professional route was for me. In prose, this may sound goofy. I know it does. That didn't change the fact that this was my destiny.

In every portion of my being, I knew that.

It's a wonderful feeling to know your destiny when it includes something you're already passionate about. At the same time, destiny has a tendency to require more work – lots more sometimes – like in this instance.

That meant one thing was for sure: that I had a lot of planning ahead of me.

In order to graduate from the doctoral program of physical therapy at Neumann University of Aston, Pennsylvania, my chosen school, I would have to complete 250 hours of volunteer service, two physics courses, and a prerequisite for psychology. That was only after the incredibly long, time-consuming, and highly involved application process was completed… and accepted.

Without a shadow of a doubt, Neumann University made it clear that it wanted its list of hopefuls to aspire for success in this field. There were no half-hearted participants allowed considering how much they made you struggle for a mere shot at it. I had information to gather, forms to fill out, essays to write, portfolios to compose. That was, as always, on top of being a successful business owner who worked full-time.

Knowing things were bound to become even more hectic if I was accepted, that took serious and careful consideration. Lots and lots of it. I was positive it could be achieved; it was just a question of finding out how.

As always though, where there's a will, there's a way. So, I had my preparation in order after a couple of sets of mental gymnastics. It was firmly locked in my mind now.

Goal Set: In 2010, I was going to be a doctor of physical therapy. In which case, I would graduate before I turned 30 years old.

Path Planned: It was going to happen, just as soon as I put the very, very, very thorough, drawn-out application together.

I can't tell you how many hours it took me to write up all the essays, fill out the forms, gather the references, and send the whole organized kit and caboodle out in June of 2006. I also can't tell you how much emotional and mental effort it took or the amount of careful consideration I gave all of it.

To a great extent, having that part over and done with was such a relief. To another, it opened up a completely new challenge as well.

Waiting.

That's always so much fun, isn't it? Waiting to hear if you were on track to achieve something you really, really wanted – in this case, my destiny – or if I was meant to reach it some other way. It's hardly something most people would choose if given the opportunity to pick something else. Yet with no other options in front of me, I had to wait. And I had to wait some more. Five months to be exact.

Finally, just days before Thanksgiving, I got the call! I was officially accepted into the class of 2010 Neumann University Doctorate of

Physical Therapy program, making it the best call ever. Even though I was in complete disbelief.

My first day, they told me, would be May 11, 2007, while orientation was scheduled for the day before.

Once again, that meant more waiting – an eternity of it! That's what it felt like. The anticipation was tough, to say the least, particularly when I was thinking about it every other moment.

The rest of my time was filled with CORE Fitness, dancing, working out, and celebrating the new year, and of course, spending time with Mom and my friends. Any space left in my schedule that wasn't taken up by sleep was spent trying to learn as much as possible before PT school: everything movement related. Oh, and I had to prepare my business and larger life for the next three years.

Is that even possible? It was going to have to be.

When I set a goal to do something, I take quite a bit of time, deliberate thought, and contemplation. I take even longer to set myself up for success.

Knowing that about myself, I blocked my schedule to get things organized and made sure I allotted enough time to complete all of my work and personal responsibilities, while leaving room to workout. Otherwise, things would not go as planned.

The first thing I knew I needed once school began was a study buddy, and not just anyone. I was looking for someone who wouldn't take himself or herself too seriously but who had the desire and commitment to put in the work and encourage me toward our mutual goal of becoming doctors of physical therapy.

But before that, I needed to find the perfect bag.

Mom always calls me a "bag lady," and she's not wrong about that. I find proper carrying apparel essential. In this case, it would have to have space for my books, binders, and papers, as well as room for all my snacks. I had to be properly fueled for sixteen hours of learning every weekend.

Last but not least in this regard, whatever bag I got had to have a spot to keep my computer safe from all the "Arianne harm" that might – and probably would – befall it. I've never been the best at taking care of my technology, old or new. Things always seemed to happen to such expensive pieces of equipment, even if I thought I was doing everything right.

I guess that's official proof I'm not a millennial?

The day finally came I'd been anxiously awaiting for so long. It felt like I was starting college all over again, including how I was equally excited and nervous.

Who would be in my class?

What would my teachers be like?

What the heck should I wear?

When you live in fitness clothes, this is always an ordeal. I wish I could be in fitness clothes 100% of the time, and I get to be pretty darn close to that considering what I do for a living. Fitness clothes are comfortable, functional, and can be modest if need be. I truly think they should be more acceptable in all settings.

Though that may be a topic for another day.

I did go with "normal" clothes: "normal" nice black pants and a "normal" casual dark green top. I even spent a few extra minutes doing my hair that morning. Normally, it's wash and go.

I'm pretty low-key when it comes to fashion and beauty. Or perhaps a better way to say it is that I have no idea what I'm doing and somehow manage to make up styles of my own.

Going into the orientation that day, I had everything I needed except for my study buddy. I even had a plan for that. For whatever weird reason, I was obsessed with finding the perfect person in this regard. I felt like it was going to determine my fate.

Was it strange? Of course. That's just me though. I knew it, and I was working with it anyway.

My study buddy was well-mapped out by the time I surveyed the potential candidates. For one thing, I needed someone smarter than me, yet calmer, who would help me stay sane if I did poorly on a test. I also needed a lab partner who would help me learn, but not do all the work. I needed someone funny or at least someone who would laugh with me, since that's all I do.

Who would ultimately fit?

The answer would have to wait.

I found a seat before things got started, then listened attentively to every word the professors and faculty members said once it did. I had to, I knew. They were talking about the next three years of my life!

My eyes did wander a bit, scoping out my future classmates. There's nothing wrong with a little recon, I figured. I could multitask with that one single additional task.

My plan was to mingle with my fellow students during our scheduled break. Though I ended up rather misusing the actual definition of that word. "Mingling" sounds so gentle, whereas I marched up to the first person on my tentative list and introduced myself in my typical bubbly, sometimes loud, and boisterous way.

"Hi! I'm Arianne. Tell me a bit about yourself."

Scott was great, and I knew we'd be friends for sure. He clearly wasn't ready for my intensity that early, and so I moved on to Allison. She was so sweet and nice but not quite the energy I needed to get me ready for anatomy and neuroscience. So, I moved on again.

That brought me to Mike, who I greeted the same way. "Hi! My name is Arianne. Tell me about yourself."

When he laughed at me, I knew right away that he was the one I'd been looking for. The study buddy of my dreams, or at least my planning.

Mike, as it turned out, was from Indiana and lived with his wife, Lauren. He seemed smart and dedicated, yet made fun of me multiple times within the first few minutes. Perfection.

This is going to work out just fine.

I was off to a great start.

The workload was incredibly intense. Yet I was inspired and excited to learn as each class went by. The more I learned, the more I wanted. I had so many more questions about what I was already doing with clients, always delighted when I could put two and two together on how many ways I could help people that I hadn't realized before.

For example, in class one day, we got into a discussion about the hamstring muscle. We were taking Gross Human Anatomy at the time, so I was able to visually link that dialogue with the classroom lecture.

Specifically, we learned about neural innervation, how your body powers itself, the blood supply, and its functions. It was all so fascinating, sending my brain racing on how to optimize its function through movement.

As we continued to discuss the hamstring's attachments to the pelvis, I quickly realized how that would impact someone with lower back pain. So, if I had a patient with tight hamstrings and lower back pain, I'd better figure out why that was happening.

But wait!

More relationships flooded in from there, since the hamstring also connects to the lower leg, which is, of course, stabilized by the foot. There were so many connections.

I couldn't just sit there and learn about the hamstring when there was so much more to learn. Why weren't we connecting everything together? What did I need to do outside of school to learn about the body as a powerful integrated unit? Would they let me take additional post-grad courses while I was still in grad school?

Probably not.

Back to the hamstring.

Fortunately, my passion for the didactic portion of school lasted all the way through. It never faded, despite – or perhaps because of – those bunny trails. Yet I wasn't sorry when it ended. Its end meant I was ready for my next step: my clinical internships.

Neumann was great in that they allowed us a lot of leeway in choosing an internship that suited each person best. Of course, they gave us a lot of options; but the final decision was up to us.

Just like finding a study buddy, I took this seriously – perhaps even more so. At that point, I had already been doing personal training for over 10 years and owned my studio for seven. For this next important phase of my education, no ordinary practice would do. I needed to be surrounded by people who would share my passion for human movement and lifelong learning. I needed a place where I could have the autonomy to explore new ways of doing things and find the best and most innovative ways to serve my patients, yet learn as much as I possibly could.

That's why I deliberately sought out Kinetic Physical Therapy in West Chester, Pennsylvania. I found out about it through my gross anatomy teaching assistant, Dr. Darren Rodia, who happened to be its president and owner; co-founder, too, since he built it from the ground up with Dr. Chris Shearer and Dr. Angelo Labrinakos.

Kinetic's reputation was fantastic, and I felt a connection at the highest level. I stalked its website, taking in everything I could online, all of which led me to believe it could be the perfect fit. From everything I could see, this place was progressive, innovative, and it focused on movement, not just treating the symptoms.

I was also very impressed with Darren himself. He was extremely knowledgeable in the field of anatomy, and I had already learned so much from him. He would help me not just memorize, say, the brachial plexus, a network of nerves in the shoulder that carries movement and sensory signals from the spinal cord to the arms and hands. He would guide me to truly understand it.

There was one other aspect that drew me to his practice. I could tell that, even though he was an anatomy expert and a businessman, he truly loved patient care.

Undoubtedly, he was very intimidating because of that combination of skills, expertise, and passion. If I had a question for Darren, say about the brachial plexus, I would prepare for hours. Just for a simple question, I would draw charts and review them over and over again. So when it came time for my interview with Darren, let's just say that I was a bit nervous.

I drove up to the West Chester location inside the ACAC Fitness and Wellness Center. You would have thought my mom would have given me some fashion tips on this one, but no. She thought I had it under control. Little did she know that I showed up in my CORE Fitness uniform – so fitness clothes. I thought I was in a gym setting and it was for PT, which in my mind is movement.

Probably not the best choice. You would think I would learn after a certain point?

The interview went great though. It was very comfortable, maybe because I was in yoga pants. We talked about goals, expectations, and even made a little bit of small talk. Then, when the moment felt right, I asked him my question about the brachial plexus.

"Darren, what would it look like if someone had a brachial plexus injury? How would it present?"

He had a ready answer to that. He also took the time to talk it out with me, and I could tell he genuinely wanted me to be successful as he did. That's when I realized this would be a good fit – and that I didn't need to be intimidated. I probably hadn't needed to prepare for hours either, though I didn't beat myself up about that one too much.

Overall, I had a great feeling that this was going to be the beginning of a great working relationship. I had a lot to learn, I knew, and he was stuck with me. On the other hand, I had passion, commitment to being the best intern I could be, and fresh ideas to bring to the table. Our mutual goal was to promote well-being through movement. Furthermore, that was his life's mission, one I could certainly respect.

Add to that how I wanted to learn as much about outpatient physical therapy as possible, and that's what Kinetic Physical Therapy did. It was definitely where I needed to be. Since he ultimately agreed, I signed on to be part of the team.

That's how Darren became my clinic instructor. He thought I was a very high-level student, which was a compliment, of course. It also meant he was going to challenge me.

I'll never forget my first day. I had 10 new patient evaluations and felt completely overwhelmed as a result, despite his confidence in me. I didn't even know how to treat a sprained ankle, let alone a rotator cuff tear. Moreover, since 10 evaluations necessitated 10 notes, I spent hours and hours learning how to do patient documentation that night.

I didn't think I'd survive the week.

But I did. I became increasingly more comfortable with my role, and Darren trusted me more and more with his patient caseload as a result. That kind of responsibility was what was best for me, and he knew it.

He always said he just needed to get out of my way so I could excel. He followed through on that to a large degree. Although he was my go-to and available when I needed him, he encouraged me to learn from all the clinicians as well, which I'm so happy he did. Every clinician brought a unique perspective, and they were all passionate about their respective specialty. I had a fantastic, well-rounded experience.

I began to assimilate all this knowledge, incorporating it with my passion for movement and lifelong learning. As a result, my clinical reasoning began to take shape. My academic curiosity was fostered day in and day out. At times, I would even disagree with Darren, though that was extremely intimidating.

He encouraged that kind of thing, for the record. I'll never forget that. He liked to say, "The smartest people stand on their teachers' shoulders, not behind their backs." I did try to live up to it, even if it took some extra nerve at times.

After having a very successful internship in so many ways, Darren offered me a job, which I was very happy to accept. I would have started right away, but I had one more clinical to do before completing all of my graduation requirements. This one was at Magee Rehabilitation Hospital in Philadelphia.

Just eight weeks. Eight more weeks, and I was a doctor.

As excited as I was to make it officially happen and start at Kinetic, I have to say I was equally excited to be a part of Magee on the spinal cord injury floor. My clinical instructor, Yasmine, was beautiful on the outside – very petite with a dark complexion and long dark hair, but there was so much more to her than simply her looks.

She was such a bright spot for all the patients, with her warm smile and kind heart. Her husband, Matt, also worked there, a fun-loving, kind-hearted guy who was just as wonderful to work with.

My favorite thing about Yasmine was her sense of humor. She was so compassionate, but truly brightened the patients' days with what she said and how she said it. That was quite the feat, considering how we saw some exceptionally tough cases.

I'll never forget this sweet lady in her mid-forties, a mother of three, who was painting her kitchen and fell off a ladder. Paralyzed from the waist down just like that, she will never walk again.

Another patient was a transgender who was prostituting in Atlantic City, only to be shot in the neck and paralyzed from the neck down. How could I forget the nice gentleman who tried to commit suicide by jumping off a building, but he survived and was paralyzed from the mid-spine down?

I had so many mixed emotions when I was there. I remember going home each night on the train feeling so down. So drained. I couldn't stop thinking about these tragic stories and patients.

When I finally mentioned it to Yasmine, I was so grateful to hear her words of wisdom. She told me I had to separate myself when I left for the day. "You can't take this home with you," is how she put it. That did help, and it was such a relief to know what I was feeling was normal.

Her advice was still quite challenging to put into practice, I'll admit. Though, she provided such a phenomenal role model along the way. I deeply admired her bright light and positive attitude that she shared with each and every patient, and I knew I wanted to do that too.

The entire experience impacted my life in so many ways, including that it reminded me all over again how blessed and fortunate I was to have what I had. It was also a powerful learning experience about life, PT, and movement in general.

The weeks passed quickly enough until the day finally came: Neumann University's graduation day: May 15, 2010.

As I sat there with my class, and hundreds and hundreds of other graduates, I remember this overwhelming feeling of gratitude, relief, and excitement. It had been a long three years, filled with constant late-night studying, making charts and guides, missed-out weddings and celebrations, early morning cramming, school most weekends throughout the year – it was an enormous life-altering commitment.

As I listened to the speakers call out each honoree, I realized I was one of those graduates. All of the things I sacrificed for the past three years paid off. I was now in a place where I could fully embrace a profession that would afford me the opportunity to live my authentic purpose.

Believe it or not, I was not in workout clothes that day. Rather, I had found the perfect classy black dress and delicate pink jewelry to accent it. I'm not sure why pink, since that's definitely not me. I think the saleswoman at the store told me it would be perfect, so I thought I would listen to her fashion advice rather than my own.

In any case, she was right.

It was a beautiful warm day, and the sun was shining bright. The people closest to me stood there, proudly cheering me on: Mom; Dad; my longstanding employees, Adam, Ashley, and Jess. Someone else I love so much was there, too. He wouldn't have missed it.

I knew my brother was with me that day. Even better, I knew he was proud.

As I was waiting patiently for my name to be called, I looked around me, taking in the sights and sounds, the newfound friendships, and the kind and knowledgeable professors who had made such an impact on my life. It all made me realize how incredibly blessed I was.

Really and truly blessed.

When I walked across the stage, shook the appropriate hands, and took hold of my newly bestowed certificate, I felt the love and support all around me. Mom cried, as always, though they were tears of joy.

She always was and always will be my biggest fan.

14

Newfound Love

One of the biggest advantages of my decision to work at Kinetic was that Darren provided me the independence to continue running CORE Fitness as well.

It was a huge decision for me to have my own company, especially as a young doctor, and I very much wanted the individuality to develop services as I saw appropriate. Seven years ago, I had started CORE Fitness with the expectation that it would be my movement discovery hub. It had turned out to be so much more than that, and I just didn't want to lose it.

How could I?

That's why I never once contemplated the idea of declining a position at Kinetic. There, I had the versatility of setting my schedule to treat patients around my duties and responsibilities at CORE. I would spend a full day at CORE – usually on Tuesdays and Friday mornings – and then treat patients at Kinetic the rest of the week. Even then though, I had time back at my home base when necessary to educate and mentor my team, do community activities, and more.

Although this seemed like – and was – quite a busy schedule in some ways, there were far too many great benefits to overlook. For one thing, my CORE family began to come alongside my Kinetic family. Darren was also developing friendships with some of my long-standing employees; and he and his wife, Janet, would attend our holiday party.

These two worlds of mine coming together gave me so much opportunity to continue spending time in the community of Delaware that I cared about so much. That meant a lot to me especially, as it kept me close to my parents and the beautiful memories of my brother.

What more could a girl like me ask for?

Professionally, it was all progressing well. I appreciated being a young doctor with so much to learn. I equally appreciated being a registered dietitian who got to use her knowledge and skills to benefit the patients she served. I'll also admit it didn't hurt to hear Darren say I was a great asset, not only to his practice, but also to the healthcare industry as a whole. He even wanted me to take on a leadership role as his West Chester branch's clinic director.

In the beginning, I tried to refuse that offer, thinking that I wasn't yet ready since I still had so much to learn. There was also the fact that I already had so many responsibilities. Still, Darren insisted. He thought I could do it, and it sounded so compelling that I gave in.

I guess he was right about that. It didn't take me long to realize that either. I could actually do this, just as he had said.

So there I was, living my professional dream, just as I had promised my brother so long ago and yet not long ago at all. In that sense, I felt good about where I was. In so many ways, I could see the improvements I was making in my own life as well as my patients'.

They would come with a wide range of pains, from their shoulders to their spines, wrists, knees, and feet; or with main complications and movement disorders caused by birth defects, injuries, lack of proper exercise, poor form with exercise, and so much more. Yet they would leave stronger and healthier, and with greater understandings of how to cope and deal with the original issue.

Human movement capabilities were really beginning to make sense to me across the board, and I loved the opportunities I got to share that wealth of knowledge.

I did realize, however, that I might have regressed a little to my former self. Not the self I'd been during my freshman year that was excessively addicted to activity, but I had to admit perhaps I wasn't leaving enough room for opportunity.

I'd been so concentrated on graduate school and on progressing my career for so many years that I had little or no time or even interest in dating. There had been several blind dates during that period that my friends and family set me up with. I had, as a result, met some really interesting people. Many of them were truly good people, too, but not right for me.

Fortunately, I realized part of the problem: I'd been meeting men who didn't necessarily fit my goals and interests or, more importantly, my values. We weren't naturally on the same page. Rationally speaking then, I determined, I could save all my future dates and myself a lot of trouble if I could only broadcast a simple idea of what I was looking for.

As far as I could tell, that meant online dating. It was either that or walk around wearing a cardboard sign with my profile on it, which seemed a little less than practical, to say the least.

In typical "me" fashion, I wanted online dating not only to be a fun venture but also a productive one. I didn't want or need a partner just for the sake of companionship, and I definitely didn't want to be with someone who would pull me away from all the things I enjoy. I wanted a real partner: someone who would support me to accomplish more and love the version of me that I loved.

Like any even slightly rational person, I never expected to find my perfect match instantly. Perhaps I was a little more confident than I should have been considering how much harder it turned out to be than I had expected.

The online pool, I found, had plenty of dates open. The issue wasn't the sea but the fish that were in it. Most of them seemed to want something far different than I did, I realized after a very short amount of time. As such, it didn't take too long before I made a rule: For the first meeting, coffee shops only.

"We can meet for coffee, and then we'll go from there," became my common response. Though even that measure didn't even spare me from a few mind-bogglingly bad experiences. For instance, after one specific date at a local restaurant, I nearly threw in the towel altogether.

Where do I even begin with that one when almost every single aspect of it was so crazy? It's just so hard to tell, but I suppose our talk about changing the oil of a car is probably as good a place as any. When I mentioned to him that I couldn't do it on my own, he made it very clear to me just how pathetic he found that admission.

"Every girl should know how to do that," he informed me, attitude and all.

To which I replied, "I'd rather pay someone to do it."

That perfectly rational, reasonable, individual response irritated him for some reason — to the point where it seemed as if he was genuinely upset. I was more than prepared to get the heck out of there after that, so I started rushing to finish my salad, evoking another needless and intensely critical response from him.

"Man, I've never seen a girl eat like that."

Are you serious?

Of course, I didn't take that as bait, but it was a moment of no comment from me. It mostly remained that way until the bill arrived.

I'm all for sharing the bill on the first date. In fact, I always offered, and this time was no different.

However, let's face it: Most gentlemen will take it and pay for it anyway.

Not this guy though. This guy was not one of the "most," and he was certainly not a gentleman. I paid the entire tab as a result!

Yet the night was still not over from there. He stepped in front of me when we eventually walked out and, instead of keeping the door open as any rational person would, he let it slam back in my face. At that point, I'm not quite sure why I was even shocked. But really?

Really?

Last but certainly not least in the long list of ridiculous, unattractive behavior he displayed that night, he even had the guts to try to kiss me. It was as if he was working from the philosophy of "negging," where men are told to disrespect women in dates or sex or relationships. Who knows? Perhaps, that's exactly what he was doing.

Regardless… Ugh!

After that one, I began to wonder if this dating idea was ever likely to succeed. Perhaps I should just quit already before I was even further behind.

Ultimately, I didn't remove my profile from the online scene and swear it off. But I also definitely didn't change my coffee-only policy. So, life and internet dating went on as-is.

Until John Shuma came into the picture.

When he reached out to me, I tried my stock beverages line on him right away. He accepted, and we scheduled a coffee date two weeks later, since that was what my schedule would allow.

Then, the day before, he reached out with a proposal to switch things up. "Look, it's going to be a beautiful day tomorrow. How about kayaking on the Brandywine?"

It felt like an offer I didn't want to reject for some reason. I answered – quite romantically, mind you, "Sure. Why not?"

We agreed to meet in West Chester, Pennsylvania, at the Four Dogs Tavern. When I arrived, he was already at the table. Better yet, unlike that horrendous date before, he stood up instantly to welcome me.

When you meet someone for the first time, particularly a possible romantic partner, it's hard not to feel at least a little nervous. I remember getting some butterflies in my stomach going into that day. When I had the opportunity to make an official, in-person first impression of him smiling at me while standing there, I realized instantly that this was going to be a totally different kind of experience.

A good one.

His kind eyes were the first thing I noticed. Next, his charming dimples and that sweet smile of his. And the fact he was tall – much taller than I was. With his six-foot-three frame, the two of us had an obvious and intriguing difference in height.

He noticed it as well, I'm sure, but he still bent down to give me a welcoming embrace from the get-go. So far, so good. There was a lot to smile about.

Even so, and despite being in a tavern, I stuck to my basic rule and ordered a hot tea to go along with my lunch. I don't regret that precaution, but I do have to fully acknowledge that changing oil and how quick or slow I ate never came up once. Our conversation flowed easily and pleasantly, as naturally as it could be about all sorts of stuff, from work to family, to our interests and hobbies.

Kayaking was obviously one of them.

He had his two green kayaks on the roof of his Jeep, while I had my little Z3 with me. We were ready to head off on our watery first-date trip after we finished eating. That necessitated that I first follow him to our final endpoint so that, from beginning to end, we would have easy transportation between point A and point B. We then rode over in his car to our starting point.

Being the gentleman that he is, John told me, "Don't worry, I'll get the kayaks."

I definitely appreciated the gesture, but I also wanted him to know that I was more than willing to help us get to our adventure, especially on our first date. Plus, when he was lowering the kayaks off the side of the bridge, the bridge itself was a little rough and shaky. So, that is when I came in. I decided to hold up the stone bridge. That's right, the stone bridge over which we had just driven. As I was using all my strength to help him as he brought the kayaks over, I recall looking at John's face full of uncertainty.

Even though he still didn't know me well, he wasn't afraid to say, "I think the stone bridge we just drove over will support me and the kayaks. But thanks anyway."

To this day, we still laugh about it.

We ended up getting the kayaks in the water and were just about to leave, John thankfully turned to me with a very important question. "Do you have your keys?"

"No," I had to admit. "They're in the Jeep."

This time, his reaction to my quirkiness was nothing short of honest, good-natured amusement. "Well, that's not going to help us."

It was yet another instance of the good laughs we got that day being together. For the record, they weren't all at my cost. Given how he almost killed me more than once with his paddles, I gave him the nickname of "Mr. Smooth."

We had such a great time and so many reasons to smile that, when our date ended just in time for me to run back to Delaware for my dance lesson, I had no trouble telling him I would love to go out again. So, we scheduled another date on the spot.

After that second one was done, we agreed to a third, which was an unforgettable affair. I was hosting my annual fundraising event, DanceSTRONG, where I was performing several dance routines. Therefore, I did have to warn him I probably wouldn't be able to hang out too much.

"But if you'd like to come, that would be great," is how I ended that somewhat back-handed invite. He came anyway though, walking in with a gray suit, white shirt, and navy blue tie, looking around to figure out where to sit.

As it turned out, he ended up at the table with my mom and her best friend, Nancy; my dad and his girlfriend, Betsey; and JoAnna, her husband, Chris, and their kids, Harrison and Bennett. Talk about a mix of family dynamics! Yet by the end of it, my family loved him, and he had JoAnna's youngest sitting on his lap, laughing like crazy, as only he can do with kids.

I'll never forget one of our best dates. How could I? John had this grandiose idea of kayaking, yet again, a 16-mile loop around Cape May Point. You heard me right, 16 miles! It sounded like a great idea to me at the time. We launched the kayaks at the Cape May canal and the ride started off beautifully. The weather was perfect, the sun was shining bright, and we even saw a pod of dolphins swimming by. It was like being in a movie. Then we saw this friendly gentleman paddling in the opposite direction of us.

He yelled over to us, "The water is getting rough out there."

We smiled back at him, looked at each other with a slight amount of doubt, and decided to keep paddling. Let's just say, that nice gentleman was absolutely correct. The water was getting so rough that it was filling up our pond kayaks, clearly not made for the ocean, with waves might I add. John warned me that his kayak was getting filled to the brim with water. I somewhat believed him. Then I heard the lifeguards blowing their whistles repeatedly while waving us in. We attempted briefly to go in and realized we would either kill ourselves or someone else with the kayaks.

As always, I set my mind to keep progressing towards our goal. I paddled as hard and fast as I could looking at each lifeguard stand as a marker. Without knowing, I was farther and farther away from John. When I finally turned around to check on him at least one full lifeguard stand length apart, he was nowhere to be found. I panicked.

"John, John!"

Nothing.

I, on the other hand, decided I was going to save him so began paddling back towards him against the current.

Then, I looked more closely and realized John was close to shore, out of his kayak and completely disheveled. By that time, my kayak flipped over me multiple times as I washed up to shore, too. Literally. I stood up with blood rushing down my leg and my bathing suit top pulled to the side. All I could do, after that show, for the entire Fourth of July crowd, was take a bow. This was one of the moments that may have bonded us forever.

I liked him very much even after such a short acquaintance; and he seemed to be trying to get to know me better, too. A good combination, to be sure. Yet I did find a couple of things that made me hesitate. Put together, they made me begin to query pretty early on, as I usually do, whether he was the right person – doubts I decided to share with Mom.

"John is nice enough," I told her. "But he does this thing where he checks out while I'm talking. We get going on a great conversation, and then I see his eyes drifting off into the distance. Almost like the lights going out on a TV."

She didn't hesitate on giving me her answer: "Arianne, you need to give him a chance. You need to tell him how you feel and take responsibility for better communication."

"I would," I protested but he really doesn't listen. I feel like there's something going on in his life that I don't understand."

My superhero mother has a rich history of giving me life-changing wisdom. So I shouldn't have been surprised that she didn't disappoint me in this case either, and I deeply thought about what she said.

It was a little overwhelming to speak to John about my issues, I'll confess, but I went for it anyway. At that time, we both knew about one another quite a bit, so I knew he had an adopted son, Kolby, whom he loved and cared for more than words could say. With that said, until I told him about my issues, I had no idea about their detailed backstory.

We sat down one night, and I asked him to tell me everything. All the details. I knew that if I understood what happened, I could support him. That's when he "came clean," I suppose you could say.

As it turned out, he had adopted Kolby to stand by a lifelong family friend. Moreover, he's been there for him, literally from the day Kolby was born. I can't go into all the details, but suffice it to say that the situation was complex – complex enough to create John's "bad habit" of checking out, which was actually about him struggling to express his feelings about the specifics.

To think that I almost let go of this incredible guy because I wouldn't have taken the time to understand him was quite an eye-opening realization. Once more, my mom had been consistently proven right, which I had no problem admitting, particularly when the results were what they were.

Because, after that, it was a fact. I knew that I loved John. For some time, I had suspected it. But after that conversation, it was official.

I was hooked.

John was the most amazing guy I had ever met. He was compassionate and funny, with infinite reserves of empathy that took me closer and closer to him. The more time I spent with him, the more I knew in every way that I loved him and the more I fell in love with him.

He was the one I had wanted to find that whole time: the one who, no matter what, loved both my good and bad and would stand by me. John made it worth all those past dates since, if I hadn't sought out online dating, I wouldn't have met him.

So when he asked me to marry him exactly one year after our first date on April 13, 2014, I didn't hesitate to say yes.

John was just as excited as I was about my continuing professional aspirations, and was quick to support my ongoing training goals. That included my decision to get my StrongFirst Gyra Kettlebell Certification, which is one of the most advanced strength and conditioning movement certifications available. It was not only an opportunity to continue to learn an ancient movement discipline, but it was a new physical and mental challenge.

It's far from simple, but I knew that it would be worth it. All the while, I had a great support system behind me, between John, Mom, and the greatest group of teammates ever in a terrific organization that made every day educational and fun.

Not to brag, but I did work with some great people. There are far too many stories to tell in that regard. They simply wouldn't all fit in a decently-sized book. But one, in particular, was especially fun in the moment and the start of something much, much bigger at the same time.

I once told Darren that, as much as I enjoyed hearing him talk, sometimes his staff meetings were a bit boring. In his defense, can any employers claim that they hold staff meetings that employees actually look forward to?

Yet Darren is the kind of leader who doesn't just talk about listening to his team. He puts that talk into admirable action, even with dumb stuff like this. That's why he launched an insane contest to spice things up after I made my little off-handed remark. Each clinic had to plan something fun and unique to implement into their staff meetings, he said. So, of course, being the dancer that I am, I suggested a dance lesson for ours.

Everyone was on board, and I was particularly excited about the part where I got to pick the song. When I chose something in the "Doo-Wop" oldies genre in honor of Dad, no one who knew me there was even a bit shocked.

That particular time, I chose Dion's "Runaround Sue." Try looking it up if you don't know it. It has a great beat that you can quickly move to. We had about 40 people in the gym, and I was teaching a swing dance to everyone: "One, two, rockstep." Everyone was laughing and smiling the whole time, including me.

Yet, in the middle of the dance, while trying to intentionally amuse my coworkers, I felt a pinpoint pinch in my calf.

It was irritating, to say the least. Luckily, however, I was a doctor of physical therapy in a room full of other specialists and doctors. So, I asked a couple of them to check out my offending limb. Honestly, none of us thought anything about it. It's not that rare for active people to aggravate a joint. As far as we could tell, there were no signs of it being anything more serious than that.

Yet something was wrong. Something was really, really, exceptionally wrong. A week or two passed by, and it seemed to only get worse, including how I found a large mass above the back of my right knee. I couldn't avoid palpating it – the PT word that essentially implies touching for exam purposes – and coming up with probable diagnoses in the process.

It must be a Baker's cyst, I concluded one day.

The next, I'd change my mind, realizing that this wasn't a Baker's cyst. It was a problem with joint capsules.

Perhaps it was a meniscus?

Then that horrible thought entered into the catalog. That life-altering, horror-inducing, absolutely exhausting thought that never led anywhere good.

Could it be cancer?

Oh, no. Oh, not that, I tried to assure myself. Possibly just some swelling of the joint.

But my brother had cancer. There was no way I could forget that. He had cancer three times. While Mom had it once.

Could it be cancer?

It can't be. Can it?

No.

But could it be?

It had to be paranoia at work in my brain, I told myself. That's what I wanted to believe, anyway. I knew for certain that the subject spawned automatic fears. It had shattered my life one too many times by then watching it literally take over David's life and affect Mom, along with other loved ones.

I constantly reminded myself that I was being unreasonable. It was just a knee injury, after all. The thought wouldn't go away, leaving me with only one desperate, desperate desire.

Please don't let it be cancer.

Please!

15

The Phone Calls

To calm my nerves and, of course, to be safe, I did make an appointment to see a physician and get properly evaluated. I knew exactly who I would contact, too: Dr. Bradley Smith. He was a great non-surgical sports medicine doctor, whom I worked closely with for mutual patients. I really respected him and his opinion, and I knew he'd be able to perform a diagnostic ultrasound to rule things out, or, God forbid, in.

During our appointment, I expressed my concerns, and he tried to give me some encouragement after the exam was over.

"It is a solid mass. So I'll need you to get an MRI ASAP. Don't worry," he told me. Then he proceeded to write me a script.

I know he sincerely meant the words to make me feel better. But it didn't. Not even close.

Solid mass?

MRI?

ASAP?

What was he saying? What did he mean? Was he inferring that I had cancer? What else could a solid mass be?

I was a wreck. That horrific C-word was racing through my head now. How could it not? I always tell my patients not to let "what ifs" take over. So why was I? Why did I immediately go to Dr. Google to go down a black hole of horrible speculation?

All the while, I was simultaneously in denial, or at least a significant state of bewilderment. My entire life and lifestyle were committed to health and wellness at the time. I had dedicated my whole career to health. So how could I possibly have a serious medical condition, especially cancer?

None of it made any sense to me.

Yet, to that, I had to remember even as I was trying to reassure myself that David was never out of shape. He was just a kid when he was first diagnosed.

How on Earth can you explain that?

Even though I knew all this, I just couldn't accept the idea that someone who follows an extremely healthy and disciplined diet, who works out regularly, who lives an active lifestyle, and who educates others on a healthy lifestyle, too, could possibly have cancer. That is to say my mind couldn't process it.

I did, however, schedule an MRI.

I was able to get an appointment very quickly since Dr. Smith was able to pull some strings. That Tuesday afternoon was anxiety-ridden, before I situated myself on the stretcher to lie in the machine. And during. And after.

Although this may sound unusual, I felt a burning sensation in my thigh when the contrast was added. Whether that was physical or mental, it was far too real. My gut knew something was wrong.

Dr. Smith knew too after he got the results what seemed to be immediately afterward. He recommended that I see an orthopedic oncologist: a sarcoma specialist, to be exact, someone who was in the top 1% nationwide for treating sarcoma.

The interesting thing is that, before I got his call, I was googling "large mass in distal thigh – female." And sarcoma came up. Not in big peer-reviewed research studies with a large subject sample, but case studies of one single person.

Despite my already intensely close associations with cancer, I had never heard of it before. Yet I didn't need to in order to know that this was not good.

Not good at all.

Mom and I went to the appointment on March 23, 2015, at Penn Medicine's Abramson Cancer Center. I felt so fearful and anxious about what I was going to hear and what I'd have to do, to say nothing about my fear and anxiety for my poor mother. I hated bringing her into this, but I needed her desperately.

Internally, we were both wrecks.

The first step was a core needle biopsy, with a very pleasant nurse in blue scrubs explaining the procedure thoroughly. She was very reassuring, and all the other nurses seemed equally wonderful, making time to smile and laugh with me.

I soon realized, however, that there would be a trainee performing the biopsy. Penn is a teaching hospital, so that's to be expected. Yet I guess I wasn't expecting it. Heck, I wasn't expecting any of this, and I had just been getting comfortable with the other nurse, too. That put me right back into full train-wreck mode instead of a moderated version.

The first nurse assured me that I wouldn't feel any pain from the procedure. But in that, she was wrong. I did feel pain – quite a bit, actually. It forced me to tap into my superpower – my diaphragmatic breathing – to keep me calm and help decrease the extremely negative sensations. I also tried to laugh with the nurses as much as possible.

We could have all used a little sunshine, I told myself.

After it was finally over, I walked out to see my anxiously awaiting mom. She had been out there much longer than anticipated, so as you can imagine she was a little worked up. I assured her that everything was okay.

It was okay.

Everything was going to be okay.

Our next appointment was with Dr. Kristy Weber, who Mom and I both loved right away. She was very professional, kind-hearted, and encouraging. She had also come from the distinguished Johns Hopkins, where Davey was treated, to now head up the sarcoma program at Penn.

She asked if I was having any symptoms, and I mentioned that I had. I told her that, for about a month at that point, I'd had a pinpoint nerve pain right in the center of my right calf. I only felt it with pressure, such as every time I sat down, crossed my right leg over my left, or crossed my left leg over my right.

"It's definitely not anything bad, but I know it's not right," is how I ended that answer.

By that point, I had already done muscle testing, nerve testing, and nerve gliding, yet nothing was changing it. It was obvious to me that this mass was pressing on my sciatic nerve.

She wasn't too concerned though. She palpated my leg and reassured us that she saw this frequently: that many times these tumors were, in fact, benign. She hadn't received the biopsy results yet, of course, but told us that as soon as she received them, she would let us know.

My mom and I were so relieved. We felt like a huge weight was lifted. The anxiety of that appointment and the run-up to it was pretty intense. So, a lessening of that enormous pressure was something to celebrate, necessitating a night out in Philly for a glass of wine, Chardonnay, our favorite.

That weekend, I had already planned to go to a continuing education course in New York. Continuing education was and still is one of my absolute favorite things to do. I know you can never ever stop learning, and I thrive on that fact and pursuit of it. So, lifted by relatively good news, off I went.

It was a two-day course to become a master instructor for Evidence Based Fitness Academy (EBFA). This was something I was especially intrigued by since I had become obsessed with feet. That may sound weird to some, but it had been quite a journey for me through knee pain, hip pain, and sacroiliac (SI) joint pain for so many years. Everyone I went to told me I had "flat feet," so I had multiple orthotics, shoes with so much support they looked like coffins, inserts for my shoes, knee braces, and SI joint belts.

I finally had an MRA for my hips, where we discovered I had bilateral labral tears, as well. Essentially that means the cartilaginous ring around both hip joints was torn, likely from poor mechanics for so long. I was even treated with physical therapy by one of my favorite professors at Neumann. Yet nothing worked, a perplexing conundrum. I just didn't seem to get better.

I realize in hindsight that there may have been some emotional pain stored in there, too. There were so many things that had happened in my life that I didn't deal with entirely. Knowing what I know now, those emotions are stored in our bodies, specifically in our fascial tissue. So, although my pain could be reproduced with movement, otherwise known as mechanical pain, I realize how heavily my emotional experience impacted my physical pain.

That is perhaps why "nothing worked." My nervous system wasn't ready for healing.

Things changed for me when I started to train for my kettlebell certification though. I had to train barefoot. There was no other option. It was expected in the kettlebell community, which led to a wonderful development in my world.

I quickly realized that training barefoot was a game-changer, emotionally and physically. The pain in my hips, knees, and SI joint started to slowly disappear. I felt more powerful, experiencing the positive impact on the rest of my body. It allowed me to begin moving in so much more of an integrated way, and without my coffins. So that's why I had to understand the science. That's why I signed up for the class.

I had researched Dr. Emily Splichal, the main presenter, for some time. She was the expert about all things barefoot and movement from the ground up. She is the Founder of EBFA Global and the inventor of Naboso Technology, small-nerve proprioceptive insoles and mats designed to stimulate the nervous system and enhance movement. I had watched hundreds of her videos, and I knew that she was exactly who I wanted to learn from. I only wanted information from the best in the field, mainly because I wanted to be the best in mine.

This particular two-day conference was geared at teaching barefoot assessments, treatment plans, and powerful movement concepts, such as how the foot is actually part of the core. I was going to learn about the interconnection of the foot and ankle with the rest of the body.

I wanted to know all of it and more.

Sure enough, the course did not disappoint. Not even close. Dr. Emily was an extremely powerful speaker, and I deeply admired her passion and expertise about the subject. I couldn't stop taking notes, as per usual; and my notebook was filled with additional comments she made along with things I wanted to look up afterward.

I was so excited after the ever-inspiring first day and I couldn't wait to call John. When I called him that evening, I was smiling ear to ear. It wasn't just about how energizing the course was. I'm sure he could feel it through the phone: my sense of relief over finally being ready to move past two years' worth of constant guilt.

For two years, every single week on our Tuesday date nights, my wonderful mother would listen to me and guide me on this major life decision: to stay at Kinetic or sell CORE. It's a wonder she didn't lose her mind with all the things I said those Tuesday nights.

One time, it would be, "I think I'm going to leave Kinetic."

The next week, "I think I'm going to sell CORE."

My patient and loving mother would just talk it through with me as only she can do, as if she had heard it for the first time instead of the 20th. Or more.

I just knew that I was burning the candle though. My whole life, I have always wanted to do a great job. I always gave 100%. Whether for my own sake or others, the jury is still out. With that said, I do know I care about people very much: my family, my friends, my patients, clients, bosses, coworkers… humanity. That can sometimes cloud my vision.

I was the director of a clinic that I loved and cared about. I never wanted to let my boss down, but I felt like I always was. I never seemed to meet my Kinetic productivity requirements no matter how many hours I worked.

As for CORE, I was only there a day and a half each week. My team was fantastic, especially James at that time. He was holding the fort down. Whereas I, once again, felt as if I was failing. I had so much guilt all the time no matter where I focused my efforts.

I was so emotionally attached to CORE though. Way more to me than just a studio, it was the primary thing that helped me grieve my brother. It helped me find my purpose. It helped me find myself. Everything about CORE was about our family, our clients, and the community we served.

It was also my identity. Everyone knew me as Arianne, the owner of CORE Fitness. I knew I did too. For 13 years, I associated CORE with my brother, my true passion, and the love I had to give.

Then again, Kinetic had given me so many opportunities. Not only that, but I also had a ton of autonomy, flexibility with my schedule, a great support system, and a great salary with benefits. On top of all that, I loved my coworkers. I couldn't have asked for more there.

With that said, I was realizing that the role of clinic director might not have been for me after all. My first and always love is patient care.

When it became clear to me that day, I felt a massive weight lifted as I said the words out loud. "Guess what? I made my decision!"

As only John could do, he asked, "About what?"

In his defense, we weren't even married yet, and he still wasn't the best listener.

"I'm going to leave Kinetic," I told him. "I'm going to stay at CORE and use it as a launch pad for a more integrative center down the road. We'll have to relocate eventually, but it will allow me to just focus on one thing and make it great!"

As John always is, he was 100% in. He started immediately talking about how we'd make it work, beginning with me switching over to his insurance. We talked for so long about all the ins and outs – way more than I can usually keep him on the phone. It felt exhilarating!

That was on March 27, 2015.

The next day at the course, inside, I was smiling ear to ear. Outside, I'm sure I looked fairly serious and deep in thought despite the fact that I was sitting cross-legged on the floor. I was loving every second and felt like I couldn't get enough. It all was making sense as she explained how the foot is our foundation. Additionally, if your foundation is poor, imagine what the rest of you may look like.

Taking it all in, I was determined to learn the information well enough to teach it myself. In fact, I told myself, I was going to become a master instructor!

As I was imagining all the possibilities of me teaching this content to fellow professionals, patients and clients alike, my phone began to vibrate in my bag. I ignored it at first, since I didn't want to miss a beat of the ongoing explanation.

This would change the way I treated patients forever.

It would change the way they interacted with their environment.

It would help them restore function, strength, and movement.

The possibilities seemed endless at that moment when my phone began to vibrate again. I really wasn't interested in it, but I figured I should at least check to see who was trying to get a hold of me.

As I pulled my cell phone out of my black High Sierra bookbag, I saw that it was Dr. Weber. Which immediately sent a pang of panic through my brain and every other part of me.

That can't be good.

That was my first thought. My second was a reminder that she'd thought the tumor was benign.

But then why is she calling?

Oh, that's right. She told me she'd let me know the actual results. So, I clearly needed to take this, which I did.

"Hi, Arianne. It's Dr. Weber."

I felt my stomach tied in knots, and my breathing grew a bit more shallow as she geared up to tell me the truth. At the same exact time, I was still processing so much information from the course, leaving me feeling both a bit distracted and tense all at once.

I quietly stepped out of the conference into the hallway, where I could still clearly hear how "gait is the most powerful assessment of movement efficiency" even though it was off in the distance now. Meanwhile, right in my ear, Dr. Weber's voice was coming through as mere sounds for the most part.

It was just one word that stood out with stark, savage clarity.

"Cancer."

Despite hearing that, "There are over 104 small nerves in the bottom of the foot," in the background, I heard that single word just fine. Maybe due to excruciating, haunting familiarity.

I tried to listen carefully to everything else she said after that, but it was so blurry. I know I must have responded in some way, but I have no idea what I said. I still couldn't tell you to this day, not with those two brutal syllables ringing in my head.

I vaguely remember her saying I would need to start radiation right away. But that was it. That's all I remember.

The phone call ended, and my phone went dark. I stared at it for a moment, still trying to process what had happened. I felt like I was in an absolute daze to the point where I didn't even know where I was.

Hearing "balance and stability" in the background was what grounded me enough that I began to make sense of my surroundings. Barefoot science began to pull me back to reality.

Speaking of reality. Could this be?

What do I do with this?

If my life were a play, the curtain would have drawn at that point. Or if it were a movie, there would have been some type of cutaway.

This was neither. It was reality. My reality. My life.

I was still right there, just as I was 10 minutes before.

Everything had been just perfect 10 minutes ago. Ten minutes before, I had been learning from one of the most brilliant minds in the movement industry alongside experts from all over the country about a topic I was so intrigued by. Ten minutes before, I had been the daughter of parents who loved me more than anything in the world. I had been engaged to the most wonderful man. I owned a successful business, and I was a clinic director at a prospering company.

I realized all of that was still true, of course. I also realized that, 10 minutes before, I'd had cancer, too. I just hadn't known about it.

The knowing changed so much though.

I broke down. The tears began to flow down my face. Almost uncontrollably. I felt this massive loss of control at that very moment.

After letting it settle in, I walked back into the course. Life must go on, I told myself as I always do. And it should go on with me doing what I love most.

With that goal in mind, I found myself getting back into my frantic note-taking pretty quickly. I thought so many thoughts, wrote way too many notes, and came up with just as many ideas. Honestly, I still managed to have way too much fun, fueled by this fire inside of me the information ignited.

The fear must have still been there. There must have still been obvious traces of leftover tears, and my demeanor must have changed. Whatever it was, it prompted this wonderful Italian man, Federico, to come over. Dark-skinned with long dark hair, he was such a gentle soul and he sensed something was wrong. So when he asked if I was okay, I told him the truth.

"I was just diagnosed with cancer."

He proceeded to give me the biggest hug that I'll never forget. Sometimes human touch – human connection – even in such a seemingly simple form can have a massive impact.

When the course ended for the day though, I had no physical human touch to rely on. I'd come alone, which meant the rest of the evening was mine: to spend with my thoughts. I had hours to think. I knew it wouldn't all be about barefoot science.

Walking back down Manhattan streets to my hotel that night was rather surreal. Everything was going on as it usually does in the city. The hustle and bustle of people in the streets, food stands everywhere, lighted signs brightening up the city.

In the same way, walking into the hotel, I could clearly see that the fountain I'd first noticed checking in that morning was still there. The hotel elevator still had the same signs, and the pleasing smell in the lobby still existed despite my world slowly crumbling apart.

Up in my room, I threw my bookbag to the side and sat down on the bed to touch my right leg where the malignant mass was. Then I just stared at it for some unknown amount of time until something struck me.

Mom.

How would I tell her? How could I possibly put her through this again?

Yet with no other choice, I vividly remembered dialing her number. Not knowing exactly what I would say, I wanted to make sure I told her in the gentlest way possible to soften the news as much as I could.

The last thing on Earth I wanted to do was hurt her or to make her worry more than she already did. So I would tell her it was going to be fine.

I would be fine.

We would be fine.

I was still going to be her silly, passionate ray of sunshine, just with a little bit of hurricane thrown in – just like I'd always been and always would be. We were going to get through this.

The phone rang quite a few times before she picked up, as it usually does. My mom rarely answers her home phone, which gave me an extra moment to prepare.

She answered, "Hi, honey. Everything okay?"

It was almost as if she knew. She always knew.

I told her what Dr. Weber told me and immediately heard her yell, "What! What do you mean?" Her voice was filled with so much panic, followed by tears.

Truthfully though, I felt like I'd heard them even before I called her.

Although I wanted to downplay it, hearing her concern reaffirmed my own fear of what was to come. I managed to get everything out that I knew, which admittedly wasn't much. I also did reassure her that everything would be okay, but I knew her heart was breaking. I felt it even though we were miles away.

Tears were rolling down both of our faces as we declared the sincerest and deepest "I love yous" possible. I always felt like Mom has been the one person with whom I can totally let my guard down, and I certainly did that night, at least to the best of my abilities at that moment.

After that heartbreaking discussion, I was on to the next excruciating call, this one to Dad. I was so worried about overwhelming him, knowing how overwhelmed he'd been with my brother's diagnoses and how he never really bounced back.

He was just as shocked as Mom was, but I remember him saying, "I'm so sorry, Oopie. Everything is going to be okay." He told me he loved me just before hanging up, and I knew he did.

As it turned out, my dad was still my dad. And my mom was still my mom. Those horrible conversations none of us wanted didn't change a thing.

Two down. One to go.

Would John still be my fiancé after I was done with the next call?

I was supposed to marry him in less than two months. How could I possibly tell the man I was completely in love with – who I'd spent the last year planning our future together – that our future was now compromised?

He had proposed to me in his backyard with a surprise Easter egg hunt almost a year ago to the day. That meant that, just 12 short months ago, I had been the happiest I'd been in my whole life.

Everything felt like it was coming together for me at 34 years old. Hearing him say he wanted to spend the rest of his life with me was truly one of the most wonderful moments of my life. Truly, there is no better feeling in the world than being excited for your future with a life partner you know you can count on.

Could he count on me now? What if I left him behind?

He knows I'll always love him. But will I be alive? Will I be there for him?

And if I were alive, would I have both my legs? Would I be able to give him children? Would I be able to give him the love he deserves?

So many negative and overwhelming thoughts were racing through my head including the excruciating question of whether he would still want to marry me after I told him what I was about to tell him. It wasn't a completely emotional question considering how my experience with cancer up until that point was mainly one of ultimate loss. I watched my brother fight as hard as he could, only to lose the battle. I watched Mr. Wortman become paralyzed from his cancer and then lose his life, too.

There was no amount of positive self-talk that could have helped me in that deep, dark sea of emotions. I felt like I was drowning, choking on all the possibilities.

The more I thought about it, the more uncertain I felt. My rational side knew his undying commitment, but logic was not in full control.

Will he even still love me?

Can he?

I finally forced myself to call him anyway, if for no other reason than to just get it over with already. Taking a deep breath, I dialed his number, feeling that same knot in my stomach that I'd felt with Dr. Weber's call.

"Hey, babe." I started crying immediately, blurted out, "I have cancer," and then really lost it altogether.

"Do you still want to marry me?" I sobbed.

Less than five seconds into the call – four of which I'd dominated so far – he relieved all my fears. "Of course, I do."

Then he proceeded to make sure I knew without a doubt that he was in it for a lifetime. He even went so far as to offer to drop everything and come pick me up right away.

I told him how much I appreciated that and how wonderful he was, but no. I wanted to stay and finish the course. That was true, but in all reality, I also needed some time to process everything.

I'm happy to say I was calmer after I hung up with him. The fear and confusion were still there, but my irrational side was a lot quieter.

John was the love of my life before cancer. He would be the love of my life with cancer. And he would be the love of my life when I beat cancer. That was how our story was destined to be.

With that in mind and needing to do something, I decided to go for a walk outside on the busy streets of NYC. Although I hate shopping, I found myself in Macy's looking for a dress for my wedding shower coming up the very next month. Sure enough, I found a beautiful royal blue dress that fit perfectly and seemed to distract me a bit and help me focus on something fun.

Somewhat.

Will I even be able to have my wedding?

I forced the question away, wanting to just focus on what I could control while I still had some to do with as I pleased. I proceeded to find a good local restaurant with an available high-top table – my favorite kind. There, I ordered a glass of Chardonnay and my favorite grilled salmon salad with olive oil on the side.

After I put my order in, I had this moment of silence that had me tearing up again. That's when I realized I had one more important call to make while I was waiting for my meal. To Darren.

Will I be able to work?

That shouldn't have been in question. I didn't want it to be in question. How could I possibly stop doing what I loved so much? I thrived off helping my patients move better and heal their own bodies.

Truthfully, I didn't know what I would say when I called Darren even though I knew I just needed to be honest. Bracing myself, I tried to be professional, calm, and reassuring when I told him the news. I think I managed for a moment or two.

Then, I lost it on him, too, crying hysterically all over again. Darren was great though, reassuring me that everything would be fine. He said he and Kinetic would stand behind me no matter what, and I knew that he meant it.

I remember sleeping well that night because of the commonality among all four calls – Mom, Dad, John, and Darren. I was assured that I was not in this fight alone.

Not even close.

At least there was that.

On March 27, I was about to take on an exciting new life adventure and on March 28, I was diagnosed with cancer. My, how life can throw you some curveballs. Just when you think you have things figured out; a new challenge comes your way. When you expect the unexpected, you're more prepared to face them head-on.

16

A Twist of Fate

I finished the course and took the train home that Sunday night to meet my first I've-got-cancer appointment with Dr. William Levin. He was a radiation oncologist since that's the kind of treatment they thought I was going to need to start right away.

Dr. Levin reminded me of a big teddy bear. He had this wonderful soft-spoken way about him and was extremely empathetic. I felt like he was genuinely trying to get to know me, asking about what I did and my interests and hope for the future.

He genuinely cared. I could just sense it.

His suggestion was for me, as a young female, was to try proton therapy due to the location of the 10-centimeter tumor in my thigh and my active lifestyle. It essentially shoots beams of protons at cancerous tissue to irradiate the problematic cells while minimizing risk to healthy tissue, as I found out.

He said it wasn't the right thing for everyone or every situation, but he believed it would be a great option for me. I didn't know anything about proton therapy other than what he'd just informed me. Mom, on the other hand, who had come with me, was so much more well-versed in cancer treatments. I think she kept reading up about more current advances even after Davey passed away.

She thought it sounded good and I trusted Dr. Levin, but we both thought we'd research it a bit anyway. Admittedly, that was the absolute last thing I wanted to do. There was so much going on in my head, and the thought of reading research articles sounded less than appealing.

Mom, on the other hand, was determined. Even though I hated seeing her there, frantically writing down notes, I'll admit that I couldn't help but expect her to be there. This didn't lessen the unbelievable amount of gratitude I had for her sitting next to me in that appointment. I truly don't know if I could have done it without her, and I do know without a doubt that I wouldn't have wanted anyone else to be by my side.

There's no one quite like your mom.

She went to every single appointment with David, and now I was doing it to her all over again. First, her son – three times – and now her other child. She had experienced so much trauma in her life, but you would have never known from how well she stood beside me.

My whole life, Mom with her comforting eyes and genuine concern, has been by my side, supporting me, filled with such love. I remember thinking at that moment how I would do anything to take this newest worry away from her.

Knowing her, she felt the same about me.

I think we can all agree that cancer isn't something anyone wants to go through. Not only is it exhausting and painful on an emotional, mental, and physical level, it's also debilitating, expensive, and potentially deadly.

Despite the common understanding of this, it's hard to describe the overwhelming nature of this before you even have your first treatment. The highs and lows, fear of the unknown, visit to one specialist after another specialist with test after test: It's overwhelming and bewildering, leaving you wondering how you're going to fit all of those extra appointments and tasks and demands into your normal life.

Can you even have a normal life anymore?

Next up was my appointment with Dr. Arthur Staddon, a hematologist-oncologist Dr. Weber referred me to. He was a distinguished older man, and it was up to him to explain in detail my cancer diagnosis, staging, and more about my treatment options.

Thank God my mom was with me for that one, too.

"You have stage 3 liposarcoma with myxoid and round cells."

Stage 3 liposarcoma with myxoid and round cells.

Stage 3 liposarcoma with myxoid and round cells?

That was apparently rare. Very rare, in fact. Dr. Staddon didn't sugarcoat much, which I was grateful for in the long run. I didn't need sugarcoating; I needed the facts, or at least I thought I did.

"How would I have gotten stage 3 liposarcoma with myxoid and round cells?"

"That's not entirely understood," he said. "But it presents itself as a mutation in fat cells."

I don't even have that much fat on my body. How could I have mutations of fat cells? Why does it have to be this? Stage 3 liposarcoma with myxoid and round cells? Why couldn't it have been a stupid meniscus tear or Baker's cyst? Or a benign tumor?

Nope. It's stage 3 liposarcoma with myxoid and round cells.

I was trying my best to listen to every word he said, but my mind was racing. I just didn't understand how it could be stage 3 when I worked so hard to be in tune with my body. Before February, I'd had no other symptoms. I was sure of it.

That visit was devastating. It was gut-wrenching, soul-searching, and nothing short of utterly horrific. I'd love to say I was able to keep it together until after we left, but that just wasn't true.

After many uncontrollable tears, I finally got to a place where I could listen again and be present. I didn't even know what my mom was doing; at that moment, all I could do was try to compose myself. That was something I really needed to do since the next hour was going to be spent talking about what my next steps would be.

Dr. Staddon's extremely qualified, professional, and kind-hearted nurse practitioner, Laetitia, was ready with information in hand. Unfortunately, that was another blow.

For a week or so at this point, I was wrapping my head around proton therapy. It would be five days a week for five weeks. That meant I'd work in the morning and take the train to treatment in the afternoon.

I was prepared to do that already and repeatedly assured by the Kinetic team that they would be completely supportive of whatever I needed to do to get through this. I might have had to make some modifications to my life that way, but I could still do what I loved.

I could still move. I could still help my patients.

I could still live!

Now, in Dr. Staddon's words, my cancer was "very rare, and it's aggressive." Moreover, "The tumor is made up of myxoid cells, which are slow-growing, and round cells, which are fast. We have research to support that round cells are sensitive to chemotherapy."

"Chemotherapy?"

What?!

I wasn't prepared for that. I had already mapped out how I would do proton therapy. How on Earth would I keep any semblance of a routine under the administration of chemotherapy?

My mind raced with ways I could make it work anyway, only for those to be dashed to pieces too. Because instead of having to undergo treatment once a week or once every three weeks like so many people I know have had to do, that wasn't what Dr. Staddon was recommending. What he thought would be best was a potent cocktail of chemotherapy drugs, ifosfamide and Adriamycin.

That last one is otherwise known as the "red devil."

Laetitia began to explain how this treatment regimen would entail four days in a row of infusions – each one about four hours long – followed by hours of infusions at night and on the weekend. As such, she suggested staying at the hospital as an inpatient five days at a time and then doing infusions on my own at home over the weekend.

Five whole days.

Well, technically seven.

Or, she went on, I could be an outpatient. That was also an option. But if so, it required my fiancé, mom, and home nurse to help me. Added to that, I would be hooked up to an IV bag almost all the time.

Considering I have always, always, always taken care of my health, rarely ever gotten sick, and never taken medications, the thought of staying in a hospital bed five days a week made me want to lose it on the spot. Again. So, I asked a bit more about the outpatient option. How would I do that? How was it even possible to do that?

"We'd have to give you a port," she told me.

A port was a device to draw blood and give treatment so nurses could access my circulatory system quickly. This would require surgery to implant part of it beneath my skin on the right side of my chest.

It's not the kind of thing a girl wants to hear a mere month or two before her wedding.

Each thing I learned sounded worse. It felt like the whole process was so very ugly in every single sense of the word, a theme that continued.

"As one of the side effects of these chemotherapy drugs, you will definitely lose your hair," Laetitia told me.

"My hair?"

A port and no hair? Karen, my absolute favorite hairdresser and good friend for 14 years, had just helped me figure out the perfect hairstyle for my wedding. We were both so excited about it, and she couldn't wait to do it for me on that special day.

Now that beautiful moment was gone – torn away by stage 3 liposarcoma with myxoid and round cells.

I think everyone has some physical characteristic they identify with and love most about themselves. Bright eyes. A warm smile. Nice abs.

Although it may seem superficial, to the person, they can't imagine themselves without it.

For me, it was, without a doubt, my hair. I loved my long blonde hair. My mom always called me a flag because of it, and everyone seemed to recognize me by it. It made me happy to look at it in the morning. Even if I was probably just going to throw it up in a ponytail, the way I saw it, it was still something uniquely me.

Besides, who wants to be bald at their wedding? You want to look your absolute best. It's supposed to be your day to shine.

With a lot of effort, I tried to resign myself to the fact that I could cry over all this "superficial" stuff when I was out of the office. For now, I had to keep listening, I told myself. And I meant it.

Except that I then realized my entire wedding might be a no-go.

"Will I still be able to get married?" I asked. "It's June 19."

"Yes," she assured. "You should be able to do that. We'll just skip a week of chemotherapy."

That made me nervous. "I don't want to jeopardize anything."

She assured me it would be okay.

That was one bit of good news, I supposed. There was also the honeymoon to consider. It was something John and I had been so excited about. We were planning all kinds of adventures, including staying at a beautiful resort.

"My honeymoon," I offered tentatively. "We're planning to go to Costa Rica. Can I still go?"

Once again, she said we'd make it work.

That was good news, too. Until I had to consider another miserable question: What kind of honeymoon would it be when I would be weak and tired, bald, and have a port?

Honeymoons were supposed to be a time reserved for married couples to truly get to know each other intimately, to kick-start their lives together, and maybe even to start thinking about having a family. Was any of that going to be possible?

A family.

John and I had talked briefly about the subject before, and I think we were open to expanding our family. If I were going to be completely honest with myself, I'd admit that I wasn't quite sure I wanted children. Regardless, both of us figured we'd have plenty of time to discuss such details further.

Later.

Except that we never factored cancer into the picture. Why would you as a newlywed? Why would you at all?

Yet there I was, next discussing fertility. As in, would I have any of that left after everything was said and done?

"You may not be able to have children," was the answer.

That completely devasted me. Just when I thought I was pulling it together, the weight of one more thing crashed down on me, and I lost it once again. I'm not sure if it was the culmination of everything or if it was that my choice was taken away. Either one was equally plausible, or it could have been both.

There had already been so much to take in, from the diagnosis to the life-disrupting treatment to the port to being bald for my wedding to now no longer having a choice to get pregnant or not. I think I was most worried about not being able to give John children if that's what he really wanted.

It was all too much.

Mom sat there and tried to hold back tears just so that she could be strong for me. But I knew that she felt my pain. She might have even been hearing that diagnosis over and over again in her head on repeat like I was.

Stage 3 liposarcoma, rare and aggressive.
Stage 3 liposarcoma, rare and aggressive.
Stage 3 liposarcoma, rare and aggressive.
Stage 3 liposarcoma, rare and aggressive.

Dr. Staddon went on to say, "You will also need to get surgery. Limb-sparing surgery. This is the main treatment for sarcoma. Dr. Weber will do this."

I felt like I couldn't take much more. I felt like I was crumbling inside.

Unlike the appointments with Dr. Weber and Dr. Levin, I felt overwhelmingly discouraged after I left. It's not at all that it was Dr. Staddon's fault; it was just a lot of information – so much of it terrible – to process.

All of it made me feel far from human.

The next appointment that Laetitia suggested was with an OB-GYN to discuss my fertility options. I was beginning to trust her despite all the heartbreaking information she had to give me that day. So, when she strongly suggested Dr. Gracia with Penn, I listened. When she told me to schedule the appointment as soon as possible, I took her seriously on that one too. The same went for starting chemotherapy soon.

At that point, I didn't know how much more tough information I could take. Considering the only other option was to completely give up and die, I told myself I could rise up and face whatever was still to come.

Even if my heart was breaking in the process.

When we finally got to leave, Mom and I sat in the car for a bit and just cried together. There was a lot of crying, actually. So much that it just didn't seem to stop. It felt out of control.

All of it felt so out of control.

That night was no different. I cried and cried on John while he sat there and hugged me in the corner of my typical spot on the brown leather couch. He didn't say much. Neither did I. But we both knew what the other was saying with our hearts.

Mine was broken, and his was breaking for me.

Truly, if it weren't for that emotional release with the two people I loved the most, I'm not sure I could have mustered up the courage to push forward from there.

17

The Power of the Kettlebell

aetitia had mentioned a local wig place or to use scarves or hats since my hair would be gone in short order. So, after much contemplation, I thought it would be a good idea to shave my head myself. That way, I wouldn't have to watch the slow, grueling process of it falling out.

Better yet, I was going to donate my hair to Children with Hair Loss, a great nonprofit organization that provides human hair replacements at no cost to children and young adults who are facing medically-related baldness. For me, that made the thought of losing my hair a joy. Some child who was suffering more than I was would get to have the locks I loved so much.

So, there we were, John, my mom, and I, at Salon Rispoli. The owner, Mario, was a total gem: such a kind-hearted soul. I was grinning ear to ear as he shaved my head while John gave me a hard time. Poor Mom, meanwhile, was a wreck, unfortunately. She pulled it together by the end, but it was impossible not to realize that this was a tough one for her.

Mario gave me the most beautiful human-hair long blonde wig though, and I walked out looking almost like myself. From there, it was off to dinner for a celebratory Chardonnay. That was a good night.

Less than a week later, however, Mom and I were right back at another appointment at Penn. Another waiting room. Another scary situation.

I had never been to an OB before. Ever. Yes, I was 34 and Mom had been telling me for years that I should find one. I always felt like my primary care physician would do, not in this case, of course. She didn't just specialize in oncology.

As I watched patients come in and out of Dr. Gracia's office, I noticed some had no hair.

"That'll be me soon," I said to Mom.

There were other patients, too. Some were pregnant, either by themselves or with their husbands.

Would I even look like myself after this?

Would I feel like myself?

They called me into Dr. Gracia's office, where there was a large wooden desk we were prompted to take seats in front of. After another much briefer wait, she came in to greet us with a very warm smile. She seemed to have an upbeat personality, too, considering the situation.

A beautiful woman with long dark hair, she was lovely and knowledgeable. As she began to go over the options, I had that same gut-wrenching feeling I had in Dr. Staddon's office. But I made sure to be present and listen carefully.

The first option was freezing my eggs. This process took at least three to four weeks, which essentially meant I would have to wait for another three to four weeks before starting chemotherapy.

Considering how aggressive my cancer was, this sounded extremely risky.

The second option was oncofertility preservation. She said that this would be done laparoscopically as part of a clinical trial. It was an experimental option. They would take the face of one of my ovaries; and then, when I was ready to try to have children, they would perform another laparoscopic surgery to reimplant the thawed tissue.

"They have had some success with this in other countries," she went on.

None of it sounded even remotely comforting: not the options, not the diagrams she drew, not the extensive information she gave. I felt like there wasn't anything I could latch onto to give me any real sense of hope. Once again, I simply couldn't hold back the tears.

While I was crying, I remember Dr. Gracia saying in a very empathic voice, "I'm sorry. I know this is hard."

"Hard" wasn't even close to describing what I was going through, surrounded by all of these life-or-death decisions. Decisions that would affect my life. My future with John. My ability to work and do what I love. My ability to move. All of it.

"Hard" didn't cut it.

It was all too much to process.

Way too much.

"So you tell me, Arianne," she said once she thought I had calmed down. "What would you like to do?"

Hard? Try impossible. How in the world could I decide? Option No. 1 meant I delayed a life-saving treatment against a rare and aggressive cancer. Option No. 2 meant submitting to a clinical trial that may or may not work. Option No. 3 was to ignore my fertility issues altogether and just go forward with that "red devil" drug and all its toxic companion drugs.

I finally turned to Mom. "What do you think?"

She immediately responded with, "Oh, honey, I don't know. I think you need to make that decision."

Three options. Yet did I really have a choice? I felt as if my free will was gone.

As I tried to hold the tears back, I took a deep breath and listened to my gut, which was telling me that my tumor was 10 centimeters. That's huge. Massive, even. It would get bigger if I waited any longer, especially another month.

I knew I needed to get that tumor out. In which case, the sure path to that was chemotherapy, then proton therapy, then surgery. So, the longer I waited, the more I delayed surgery and the more I increased my odds of becoming an amputee.

I needed my leg. It was everything to me. The last thing I would even want to think about was losing it, which used to be the normal treatment for sarcoma, I'd learned. It still is necessary in many cases, but not like before, evidently.

After several breaths in and out, I answered Dr. Gracia as confidently as I could. "I'd like to do the oncofertility preservation."

I want to start chemotherapy as soon as possible.

Who says that?

Dr. Gracia nodded. "Okay, Arianne. We'll get you scheduled as soon as possible."

Before I knew it, I was scheduled for surgery, and on the same Friday, I was scheduled for my port placement.

Was that even possible? How could I have two surgeries on the same day?

Up until then, I'd had zero surgeries except for my Mohs procedure for skin cancer years ago. I'd never been on medication stronger than an antibiotic from my family doctor either. Yet there I was about to have two surgeries in one day in order to spend the next eight months of my life on heavy-duty drugs.

We left the appointment partially in shock and once again sat in the car and cried together. And cried. And cried.

"When will things get easier, Mom?" I asked her.

"I don't know, honey," was all she could reply.

Easier wouldn't happen for a while, as it turned out. It certainly wasn't there less than a week later when I was standing in a hospital gown ready for surgery. The sun was out, the birds were chirping, and the sky was blue. Yet it felt like I was standing in front of an insurmountable mountain with the darkest clouds hanging over my head and predators lurking in every shadow.

It wasn't that I doubted I would come out of this totally fine. I knew I would, even then.

I just wished I didn't have to go through it at all.

Surgery seemed to go fine, according to Dr. Gracia. General anesthesia, however, not so much. I was a complete disaster afterward. I couldn't stay awake once I was out and in the recovery room. I'm sure it was a combination of things: I was drained, grieving, and under heavy medications. I was in there much longer than expected regardless, leaving my parents even more worried about me.

Yes, they both came that day. I remember barely directing them in the car to my next appointment, which was funny. I was so delirious, but between Mom's lack of direction and my dad not feeling his best, I seemed to be the best person to get us where we needed to go.

In my more coherent moments, I remember my heart breaking for the two of them.

I'm so sorry, Mom. I'm so sorry, Dad. For all of it.

I also remember hoping they didn't kill each other. Dad wasn't doing well at that time, especially with my diagnosis. I was always so worried about him and how he would respond. He tended to turn to alcohol at times like this, a habit that was taking an obvious toll on his health. He was having a hard time walking and breathing, two of our most important functions in life.

He loved me, though, and was determined to be there that day. So, instead of worrying about me surviving the day, I was worried about him surviving the day.

"I love you, Oopie."

"I love you, too, Dad."

After rushing through the city, we made it to Pennsylvania University Hospital for the port placement; where they naturally gave me more anesthesia. I was so loopy when I left that day, I didn't know what happened to me. I felt like I was run over by a truck. I was pained, constipated, bloated, sore, exhausted, and I had an immense loss of mental clarity.

I went to bed that night inundated with the worst emotions and sensations. I was terrified, confused, angry, sad, and still not quite right from the drugs.

This was only Day 1. Chemotherapy started Monday.

I wasn't even remotely recovered by then, especially when this wasn't just any chemotherapy. It was one of the most aggressive cancer treatment combinations that medicine had to offer, designed to meet the severity of the cancer that was trying to take my life.

I had opted to do outpatient chemotherapy mainly because I didn't want to be in a hospital bed. I wanted to maintain some normalcy. Truthfully, I wanted to be able to work out still, and I really thought I could.

Little did I know how horrific this would be.

At least I was greeted by some of the sweetest nurses on the fifth floor of the Farm Journal building. They were so kind and seemed to be able to answer all my questions and then some. They took my blood, weighed me, and got my vitals, then got me situated in a big comfy green chair – a recliner to be exact. I had brought my white, fluffy blanket, some snacks, and a stuffed animal from my eight-year-old almost stepson.

Just before I started treatment, Kolby had done one of the sweetest things in the whole world. It was a complete surprise when he took me to Build-a-Bear and picked out an Incredible Hulk bear because he said I was brave and strong. As such, that stuffed teddy was coming with me to this. I needed all the strength I could get.

The first infusion I got was the red devil I'd been warned about. I recognized that right away. It was impossible not to. Chemotherapy is poison, designed to kill anything it touches over time.

The hope is simply that it kills the cancer cells before it kills the host.

Even so, the first day wasn't so bad. I felt exhausted, but not too terrible. So, after hours of treatment, Mom and I made our way home. I had a little break for a couple of hours before being hooked up to more infusions for the evening, and John was planning to meet us there so he could help.

I was even able to get in a quick kettlebell workout and a short walk that first day. Yet, it got harder from there.

Mom came to the hospital with me every time. John came over every night after chemo to help with my many infusions. He would drive to the city to meet me at treatment sometimes, too. I appreciated their efforts so much, but watching them interact during this phase was tough. They were so stressed out and sometimes would argue about how to clean my port.

There were times I honestly thought they might accidentally kill me.

Chemotherapy was no joke. It's debilitating. Each day that went on with it left me weaker and weaker, more and more nauseous, and more and more exhausted. I essentially felt I was dying. I'd work out Mondays, go for a walk on Tuesdays, and then fall apart until the next Monday.

Throughout it all, I tried to be as strong as possible. Physically, that felt entirely impossible most days. I did somehow begin to find my mental strength again. I didn't cry as I did before treatment. I knew there was a plan. Things were seeming more in control.

Honestly, there were some challenging moments still. More than I'd care to admit. I knew how hard it was for my loved ones, so I tried my best to be silly and laugh with them whenever possible. For example, if they forgot to clean my port with saline, I'd tease them that they were trying to kill me.

At the same time though, I definitely began to question if doing outpatient was the right decision. It was so much for them.

Maybe I have to accept that "normal" just isn't an option anymore.

I would gain more and more weight as the week went on, looking worse and worse in the process. About 10 pounds of extra fluid isn't attractive on anyone. It wasn't comfortable, either. I would have to wear special baggy clothes because I wouldn't fit in my usual clothes.

I knew he didn't care, but I hated that John had to see me like that.

Not to mention how I was bald, eyebrow-less, eyelash-less, exhausted, and weak. I almost constantly had infusion bags attached to my chest. I avoided mirrors as much as possible, too disturbed at the sight in them. As the weeks went by, I was sitting in my chemo chair more often than not.

That chair was supposed to be my favorite chair: the one I'd sit in with Mom and watch Lifetime movies in. The only chair that my beloved brindle puppy, Zoey, was allowed on. It was supposed to be a symbol of relaxation, not of anguish.

I was always covered up in blankets, too, because I was always freezing. I felt weak and I looked weak, like a cancer patient.

Like my brother had been.

Oh, Dave, is this how you felt?

That realization was overwhelming. That this... This was what he had gone through. Even though I'd tried to deeply empathize with him, I knew that that wasn't possible unless you were going through it yourself. I had known it was terrible all those years ago; I just hadn't realized how much so.

Now I finally understood on a deep, personal level how it felt to experience all of it along with the pain. And embarrassment. And the fear.

Every Friday after my four days of chemotherapy, I would head over to John's house for the weekend. We weren't married just yet, so I was still living with Mom at the time. It sure wasn't like the weekends we used to have. I would pack my port attachments in the trunk of my Z3 and drive there in a daze.

Perhaps I shouldn't have been driving at all?

I would walk in, bags in hand, drop them on the floor, and start crying. I was so depressed every Friday. I had never felt that way in my whole life.

John always had the same reaction though. He would just stand there and hug me. Then one day, I'll never forget, he said to me, "No one ever said this shit was going to be easy."

Boy, did that make me laugh. So, of course he continued to use that line every time I needed a smile.

Then there was my sweet Kolby. He was so genuinely concerned about me and would come to ask questions about cancer, chemo, and how I was feeling. It made me sick that he had to see me like that. The reality was I couldn't get off the couch once I sat down. I wasn't strong enough to get off the couch.

Or was I?

Sure, I felt like death. But really?

It hit me one day. That supposed reality I'd accepted. *I'm not strong enough to get off the couch.* Had I really just thought that? I was a fitness competitor, for crying out loud! I was a Miss Delaware runner-up. I was kettlebell certified. I was a physical therapist.

Movement was my life.

At least it had been, my body reminded me. The defeated part of me was quick to add that it wasn't anymore. *I wasn't anymore.*

Nevertheless, not that long ago, I was. I was strong enough to deadlift one and a half times my bodyweight. I could do a hundred 16-kilogram kettlebell snatches in five minutes.

And now I'm not strong enough to get up from the damn couch.

Did it have to be that way? Perhaps I could claim my life back after all, I began to wonder.

Those thoughts led me to begin the journey of understanding the ins and outs of my condition. I wanted to comprehend in some small way what my diagnosis meant. Dr. Google, of course, goes right to the language of survival and survival rates. There had to be more than that though.

I was sure of it.

There are only 12,000 cases of sarcoma a year, I already knew. And it resulted in a 50% survival rate. Fifty percent.

"Survive" is a horrible word, I'd discovered so many days ago though. "Survive" implies barely making it through. It means staying alive and nothing more.

In my whole life before that point, I had never just "survived" anything. I'd experienced, and I'd overcome. So why would I simply "survive" cancer?

Forget that, I decided. I wanted to thrive! And not like I'd done in the past. Not like the things I had overcome. I wanted more.

I wanted to live!

I wanted to keep rising. To keep reaching. To keep growing my abilities and my knowledge and myself in the process. That was me before cancer, and that could be me again.

When should I get started?

Although my gut, which I always trusted, was screaming, "Now!" I made the decision at my worst part of the week. Although I didn't go work out that very second, I changed my mindset right then and there. I made a plan, relying on the old me – the real me – who was all about commitment and follow-through. Once I made a plan, there was no turning back.

It went like this…

Mondays were "getting back to life days." I had to navigate past the IV fluid stage over the weekend, then fuel up on some tasty pizza on Sunday with John after barely eating all week. Then I was going to be ready for work Monday, meaning I was going to go get a good workout in, and not just any workout.

Kettlebells.

Why kettlebells? For so many reasons, part of which can be explained by their name. The term first appeared in Russia in 1704 and originated from the Persian word *gerani*, meaning "difficult." If I was going to prove myself above and beyond this whole cancer "thing," I might as well go all the way.

There was also the fact that I was Russian kettlebell certified – StrongFirst Gyra Level 1 and StrongFirst Gyra Level 2 – before the sarcoma. I was still certified during, just like I would be after. I worked my ass off to gain that accreditation. It took years and years of training, filled with both triumphs and failure, too.

That was exactly why I was going to get myself to the gym and do kettlebell deadlifts, goblet squats, swings, Turkish get-ups, and farmer's carries. Because I could.

Some may have said I was a bit obsessed with kettlebells as my primary means of fitness. Johanna, chemotherapy nurse practitioner on the inpatient chemotherapy floor definitely would have agreed. There I was that Monday, walking in with my hat to cover my hairless head, my healthy food, my cozy blanket, and my kettlebell.

Looking at the latter, she attempted to be respectful as she asked, "Is that a kettlebell?"

"Yes, it is."

"I'm not sure I've ever seen that here before," she noted.

My guess is that she was probably right, and understandably so. Looking back though, the kettlebell represented much more to me than a fitness tool. It also represented power. As long as I was holding that kettlebell, cancer would have no control over me.

When I finished that first workout, I was fairly depleted. I certainly didn't feel empowered after that workout. I didn't feel fearless. And I didn't feel like a survivor.

But I did feel like me. Plain old me. The one who thrives on movement.

It was the first step in taking my life back.

My next was to remember just how much I loved being a doctor of physical therapy. I loved every opportunity to help change people's lives through the power of movement. How could I not love that? So many of my patients hadn't been able to get on my extremely decreased schedule.

That was going to change, I decided, opening up my schedule for as many of them as my body could handle. I drew strength and power from treating them, which meant I wasn't being foolish or ignoring my condition by getting back to work this way. I was providing myself with much-needed therapy.

Soon enough, my schedule started filling up with old faces and new faces. As it did, I felt more and more like my old self.

That meant I'd made two steps forward – a great start.

There was yet another obstacle I had to work through though. This whole time, I felt so bad for John. He hadn't signed up for this, and I was constantly feeling like I couldn't be the woman he wanted or needed me to be. He was always so stoic, but I knew the whole thing was exceptionally hard for him nonetheless.

Fear can be all-consuming if you let it be. It has a way of dominating everything if we let it have free reign over our lives. So, sure enough, all of my worrying about John led me to forget something so important: that I loved John more than anything in the world and couldn't wait to spend the rest of my life with him.

I forgot in all of that chaos that being his bride was what I was dreaming of.

Once I remembered all of that, I also remembered we had a wedding to get ready for. John still wanted to get married and stick to our original timeline, which was only a little over a month away. My mom, on the other hand, was a little apprehensive until she remembered that the doctors thought that getting married could be a positive light during a very challenging time.

Fortunately, at that point, I had already spent an entire year planning every intricate detail of it, from creating handmade wedding invitations to making all the table decorations and everything in between. I loved every second of it, I might add. Sure, I still had some confirming to do: times, places, people, attire, vendors, and the guest list. But I knew it could all come together as I'd imagined.

As it turned out, we had almost 300 people that were planning to attend! It was amazing.

John was amazing. Our love was amazing. It was time to celebrate as we deserved.

18

A Light in the Darkness

I was on cloud nine when I woke up that beautiful June day, and the sun was shining bright in return. Three brutal rounds of chemotherapy were behind me and I felt so light and joyful, uplifted, and completely in love.

As per usual, I wasn't really worried. I had spent a whole year preparing and planning, so I was ready to accept whatever was and would be. I was mainly excited about the day to come, which was already looking pretty picture-perfect.

We had chosen Brandywine Manor House, located in the heart of beautiful Chester County, because it represented us so well. It was a beautiful, serene, rustic lake venue with a beautiful barn. As much as we both loved nature, it was totally us.

My bridal party and I were getting ready together, and I couldn't help but feel how grateful I was surrounded by such beauty and kindness.

My future mother-in-law, Nana, looked gorgeous in her taupe gown. When she hugged me, she teared up. She was so happy for both of us, and I felt every bit of it in that embrace. I loved her and my father-in-law, Gaga, so much. They are two of the most special people in the world, and

I felt so lucky to be warmly accepted into their loving family. John's sisters, Alicia and Danielle, were at the wedding too, and I could not have been happier to have them by my side.

They were crying frequently – especially Alicia – and I knew how happy they were, too. I couldn't wait to call them sisters for life.

Also with me were my soon-to-be nieces, Julia and Emmie. They kept giving me hug after hug in their lovely teal dresses with their hair all done up.

Of course, there was JoAnna, David's girlfriend, who never deserted him or our family throughout his illness and ultimate passing. She'd been like a sister to me for years now, so there was no question she'd be a bridesmaid. She was always by my side.

My college roomies: the lovely, curly-haired Leah with her big, beautiful smile and Rachelle, playing some kind of funky music complete with lyrics that were a little… ummmm… let's say attention-grabbing. They were making sure I was smiling the whole time just like we used to do back at the dorm. Their contagious spirit and unique ability to liven the room were evident.

My bestie, Kristin, was there too. She was my maid of honor. I loved her so much and we had been through some trying times together. Me losing my brother; her losing her parents. We had traveled the world together and bonded on such a deep level, and I was so blessed to have her by my side.

As we all got ready, cocktails were going around like wildflowers, which definitely didn't hurt.

Karen, my friend and hairdresser, was a guest at the wedding but also had an enormous job. She was charged with making my wig look perfect. Our ultimate goal was to make it look like my real hair would have: long, blonde, and pulled to the side for my veil to fit as we'd first planned out months ago. I knew she could do it.

Besides, it was probably a better job than the makeup artist who had to make sure I had natural-looking eyebrows. I happened to have a few straggling eyelashes that we were able to work with.

Not quite a Maybelline look, but hey, it worked.

And my hair? Oh my word, my hair. After Karen worked her magic, I looked in the mirror and nearly cried tears of joy. It was stunning, and most importantly, it looked like me. I couldn't stop thanking her over and over again for being such a big part of my day.

I didn't have to worry about a thing that day. As it turns out, Allison – one of my longest-lasting friends and bridesmaid extraordinaire – made sure everything was perfect. She ensured that all the details were just right and just how I wanted them in her typical take-charge motherly type of way. Even my dear friend and old CORE Fitness buddy, Stacy, was there capturing every special moment of the day with her incredible photography.

Of course, there was Mom, looking beautiful as ever in her bronze-colored gown. As we were about to take a picture, she held my hand and we stared at each other. The love was pouring through both of us, and I could see how happy she was. How proud she was. I felt this deep sense of gratitude toward her for helping me through everything.

John's groomsmen were nothing short of extraordinary as well. His best friends, the guys that had stood by him through thick and thin were standing beside him again that night: Dano, Jeremiah, Jason, Matt, Kosh, and then as best man No. 1, Kolby.

I was so touched by Kolby that day. His love and genuine concern were so precious. I knew he was worried about me, but I also knew this was a big change for him. I was coming into his life that he had built with his dad.

He came into the dressing room multiple times just to check on me, just to see how I was. Each time, he wouldn't fail to ask, "Need anything, Arianne?"

It brought another several rounds of joyful tears my way.

Teddy was best man No. 2. And boy, was he not one of the greatest guys? He and John had met in the Air Force, and they'd been best friends ever since. I had already appreciated Teddy from when we first met, but my wedding day took it to another level.

He had made a point to tell me that he wanted to talk to me, just the two of us, before the wedding. Apparently, that was to tell me, "Arianne, I've never seen John so happy. I think you're the best thing that ever happened to him."

By the time the brief but heartfelt talk was through, he had tears in his eyes. All I could do was simply hug him. Words couldn't suffice when I knew how important Teddy was in John's life. Of course, his tears made me cry, too. It was such a beautiful moment, and I realized even more that all of this felt so right.

His comments were still on my heart when the wedding was about to begin. Surrounded by so much love, I knew I was about to walk into a room filled with even more love, straight toward so much more of it.

This was the big moment. The moment I'd been waiting for. Dad was going to walk me down the aisle. He was waiting outside the room, looking quite frail and nervous, yet handsome and proud.

"You look beautiful, Oopie."

"Thanks, Dad." I smiled big at him. "I love you."

He had some pretty significant health issues by then due to his longstanding relationship with alcohol. Yet I also knew he'd been practicing for months to make sure he could physically be there for me today and walk me down the aisle, as well as have our Dad-daughter dance.

Although my father might have been an alcoholic, it never took away from how much I loved him, even in the darkest of times. Like when his drinking ended his marriage with Mom. Like when I didn't hear from him for almost a year after David passed away. Like when he came to my surgeries after I was diagnosed, and I was more worried about him than myself and my condition.

I knew how many wonderful qualities he had, too. Like how he was my dad. Like how I knew that he loved me. Like the fact that I knew how proud he was of who I was and what I'd accomplished. He always rooted for his "poochie." And he was here now.

There was no doubt that alcoholism was slowly taking his life, but he made sure to be there for me on my wedding day. He knew how much that meant to me.

That meant the absolute world to me.

Our cue came, arms hooked together, and we began walking in the gentle mist of rain. I was beaming as everyone smiled at us while we made our way down the aisle… to where my wonderful almost-husband waited for me. I gave Dad a little extra support along the way, but no one would have ever noticed.

I couldn't stop grinning from ear to ear.

When I heard John read his vows, it solidified the beauty of this relationship. For someone who I wasn't sure even listened and was so private about his past, his words melted my heart and everyone else's:

Just when I thought I had everything figured out,

You walked into my life and taught me so much.

You taught me to laugh at all life's challenges.

You taught me how to open up my heart and soul,

And you filled them with more love and compassion than I ever knew was possible.

You taught me that regardless of how hard I work, you will always work harder.

I admire your dedication to help others and your kindness to all those you meet.

Your courage and strength inspire me every day.

The world is truly a better place because of your presence.

I vow to love, encourage, and respect you.

I vow to trust and value your opinions and stand by your actions.

I vow to listen to your advice and occasionally take it.

I promise to give you all my love and to keep you smiling.

I promise to create a life for us of unexpected and crazy adventures.

I promise to keep you prepared and to fix everything you shall break.

I always say that I have never had a bad day,

Now with you by my side,

I know that will always stay true.

I am excited to walk hand in hand throughout the rest of our lives together.

I give you my hand, my heart, and my love from this day forward for as long as we both shall live.

I can't tell you how touched I was when Father Greg finally said, "You may kiss the bride." I couldn't contain myself any longer. Throwing my arms up and around him, I hugged him so tight, exclaiming, "Yes!"

That day was exactly how it was meant to be. It wasn't about cancer, not even for a moment. It was about us and the life we were going to build together.

At the reception later on, Mom gave such a beautiful and loving toast to John and me. I knew by her words and the look on her face that she could not have been happier for the two of us.

Kristin's speech, of course, was one-of-a-kind. It was filled with stories of our crazy adventures to New Zealand and Hawaii, and all the trying times we'd been through together that showed our bond for life. It was so much stronger than anyone could ever imagine.

Teddy's speech, meanwhile, was so heartfelt that everyone, including me, cried.

Shortly thereafter, I noticed that all my guests were wearing something in common. Despite being dressed in various suits and dresses, ties and earrings, and shoes of varying colors and fits, they all wore the same thing around their wrists: the same royal blue "Challenge Accepted" bracelet I was wearing myself. It was a gift Darren had given me at the start of my cancer journey to encourage me to get through all this mess. John had made matching ones for all my guests, just with "AMS 2015" written on the other side.

As per usual, it took me a while to figure that out, especially with dancing to be done and people to thank and hug. When I finally asked John about it, it turned out that he'd had all the groomsmen hand them out earlier – making for the most beautiful touch to a day that was already so magnificent.

Another standout moment that day was my dance with Dad. He took quite a bit of time to pick out the perfect song, but finally decided on, "Daddy's Little Angel" by Tony Carter.

As we dance, I keep our love deep within my heart
And thank God for giving me this angel in my arms…
You're my little angel
So baby, don't you cry.
It's time to spread your wings and fly.
If there's one thing this father knows
The hardest part is letting go.
But you will still always be…
Daddy's little angel

As the night began to wind down, I reflected on that and so many other special moments. The handmade cake by Nana. The blissful music. The hugs from Kolby. The toasts by my mom and closest friends. The beautiful outdoor lake setting. Such strong support from friends and family. And John.

Always John.

I had just married the best man in the world, and I knew that we would live happily ever after together. Life was starting to look truly great again.

19

Challenge Accepted Indeed

Just after my honeymoon, where John and I didn't miss a beat, I flew to Florida to receive a distinguished award: the "2015 Sports Medicine Specialist of the Year" by the National Strength and Conditioning Association. It couldn't have come at a better time.

Although I was still a bit immunocompromised, I figured if I could have a wedding with over 300 people, travel to Costa Rica, and go surfing, ziplining, hiking, and horseback riding… then I sure as heck was going to receive that commendation in person. With all that I had dedicated to my profession, the fact that I received this during one of the most challenging times of my life was nothing short of amazing.

Things were definitely looking up.

I finally had decided to sell one of the loves of my life, CORE Fitness. Considering I was working and now living in PA, with cancer might I add, this seemed to be the best decision. I continued to work at Kinetic which was absolutely the best choice I could have made at that time in my life.

There was quite a bit of planning to do though. Finding a buyer for something that you loved so much was no easy task. Interviews, meetings, legal and accounting responsibilities filled any additional time I had.

Although this was not what I had planned just a few short months ago on March 27 when I called John with utter excitement, I felt at peace. This was exactly where I was supposed to be and the planning for the last and final holiday party was in place.

Along with my new outlook, my extreme passion for movement was revving up again, too. I loved to move. I needed to move. To me, it was a gift, and it's never let me down at any other time in my life. So why would it now?

After kettlebells helped me get back in the groove, I did consider just working out normally from there. I didn't need to go overboard. I needed enough to help me get stronger mentally and physically. That was technically it.

But that isn't what I would have been doing before cancer. It sure as heck wasn't going to stop me now. So, I decided to push myself a bit harder at a nice, healthy pace – Arianne-style.

A challenge had been issued.

A challenge had been accepted.

As I mentioned previously, I wasn't about simply surviving cancer at that point. I intended to thrive through and well beyond it. Based on that ambition, I couldn't think of a better time to take on the greatest movement challenge of my life. The ultimate movement challenge.

American Ninja Warrior.

It's a competition based on the Japanese television series *Sasuke*, which features hundreds of competitors attempting to complete obstacle courses of increasing difficulty. There are various rounds in various cities across the United States, all aiming toward the national finals where the "American Ninja Warrior" is determined.

The competition requires lots of movement skills: agility, strength, flexibility, cardiorespiratory fitness, endurance, and power. That's not even all of it. It's one of the country's toughest obstacle courses.

So why not start now in the middle of cancer treatment?

It did cross my mind to hold off until I had regained some strength, but that thought passed quickly enough. I had just finished chemotherapy and was now moving on to proton therapy. Although the chemo did kill the round-cell component of the tumor, the tumor itself had increased in size. That sounds bad, I know, but I can't lie: I was looking forward to having a break from chemo.

I still had to finish my other three rounds eventually, just not now.

I had already scoped out this local gym in West Chester, Pennsylvania. I'd been eyeing it up for a while for a few reasons, including its name: iCore Fitness, which was very familiar for obvious reasons. As such, this "ninja" gym felt like it was meant to be.

This was happening.

Since I was having radiation treatments five days a week in Philadelphia, I would take the train each day from Exton to 30th Street Station, then walk from there for about 20 minutes to the hospital. Afterward, I'd walk again to the train, a length of streets and sidewalks I always used to clear my head.

The first time I went to the gym afterward was a Thursday, and I couldn't wait to get there. The excitement was killing me! The suspense!

The moment I walked in, I was greeted at the door with a huge grin by an employee named Cajua, who was more than happy to sign me in. Taking in the actual interior as he did, I immediately saw the huge warped wall in the back and the bright lime green color accenting the place is one of my favorites. It felt so motivational right from the beginning.

Cajua directed me over to the owner, Mark Falcone, who was obviously busy. Yet he stopped what he was doing and made a point to chat with me for a few minutes. It was apparent how passionate he was about this relatively new sport.

"Hi, my name is Arianne. I'd like to train for *American Ninja Warrior*."

"Awesome!" was his instant reply. "Let's do it."

"Well, I do have some things going on," I cautioned him. "I just finished chemotherapy. I'm currently in radiation. I have surgery scheduled for my leg in September, and then I have a few more months of chemo. So we'll just need to work around some things."

That didn't deter him though. "Let's start Tuesday."

So, before I knew it, there I was with an extremely talented and passionate trainer to help me prepare for this latest challenge of mine. And it was quite the challenge. On the one hand, Mark was very accommodating in his approach. On the other, we both had the same goal in mind: to get me ready to submit my official application for the show.

We had to get moving. No slacking allowed.

Sometimes Mark would work out with me, which was a blast. He clearly was much stronger, but his approach was so supportive and encouraging. He had so much faith in me that I'd get there too one day.

Sure enough, I could see myself improving each week. It was just a tiny bit at a time. It was still most definitely there.

We started with grip work, where I had to hang from bars and objects of all sizes and shapes. Then we moved on to swinging while hanging before tackling obstacles – again, many of which involved hanging.

The rope jungle. The devil steps. The salmon ladder. Gymnastics rings. The possibilities were endless. So many things to learn! I went to the gym most days of the week, going in and leaving alike, with so much energy and strength as a result. I'd work on whatever Mark told me to work on. Then I'd go home and show John the progress I'd made – with a ton of excitement, I might add.

John was always so enthusiastic for me that I'd light up even more. I knew he believed in me; but when he'd say, "Wow, baby, that's amazing," there was nothing like it.

I loved being able to surprise him with what I was learning and achieving. Heck, I loved surprising myself!

It was such an incredibly inspiring journey. Movement and fitness always are. When you continue to challenge the complexity of the human body, there's always more to learn and grow and heal. So even though I'd been moving my entire life, this was a whole new world to explore.

In the heart of all that, something else remarkable was happening. Not only was my body starting to get stronger and fight back against the horrific disease that had taken so many lives and had tried to take mine... I also felt my old self coming back. I was winning in every way possible too: physically, emotionally, and spiritually. It was so incredible just how great I was feeling.

This next statement is not one made out of pointless pride. It's an encouragement to any of my readers who are struggling with anything, cancer or something completely different. I felt great because I did everything in my power to feel great. I didn't cut any corners in this quest. I had micronutrient testing done to make sure I was eating in such a way to heal my body and support what it needed during that time. When John taught me how to fish on the kayaks, I realized how important mindfulness was as well. I learned how to find stillness in my mind and my body amidst the storm. Responding to the daily challenges of cancer treatment with clarity and creativity became more the norm, rather than reacting with frustration and anxiety. It wasn't something that just came naturally, however, it has to be cultivated over time.

I did have my intended surgery scheduled for September 15. The surgery that could have so easily been an amputation. Yet thanks to advanced treatment options and research, it was a limb-sparing procedure instead.

My DanceStrong fundraiser event was scheduled several days before my surgery. There wasn't a chance I would miss one of my favorite nights of the year to honor my brother and raise money for cancer. At that point, my skin was extremely irritated, and my leg was swollen from radiation, but Val, my fantastic dance teacher, was able to modify my routine to make it look elegant and seamless. It was the most well-attended fundraiser to date. With my wig on and my flowy white gown, we performed a beautiful lyrical routine to "Fly" by Celion Dion.

I felt stronger than ever going into it, so I knew I'd bounce back.

Afterward, I stayed overnight in Penn's hospital. They were adamant about taking me out in a wheelchair the next day because that was hospital policy. I, on the other hand, was adamant about walking out of there. And I won.

After Dr. Weber removed an 11-centimeter tumor from my sciatic nerve, artery, and vein, while also digging into my hamstring muscle, I walked out.

I walked out.

Because I could.

After watching my brother have that gift of movement taken away, I wasn't about to take that capability for granted.

I wasn't headed to the gym for a little while anyway. But John, as a surprise, built me my very own *ANW* gym in the basement, equipped with cannonballs, pull-up bars, and rock-climbing holds. So what did I do while I was rehabbing my leg? I could still use my upper body after all.

When I returned back to iCore, Mark said I was doing great. Better yet, he felt like I was ready to take my fitness journey to the next level.

Those words spurred me on to see exactly how good I really was. Because why not? So, I filled out my official application for *American Ninja Warrior* and sent in my video submission the very day my chemotherapy treatment officially ended on December 3, 2015. I was sitting in the hospital bed, feeling my absolute worst physically; but when I hit that submit button, I remember feeling a sense of power.

I couldn't think of a better date to apply.

I knew it was a long shot. Everyone told me that, especially after hearing that my entry was one of 80,000. I had already climbed one mountain, so I knew that nothing was going to stop me from experiencing everything life had to offer, one way or the other. *American Ninja Warrior* or not.

Challenges were bound to come, but I was determined to rise above them.

20

American Ninja Warrior

*A*t approximately eight o'clock in the evening on May 11, 2016, I got the call; not a dreaded call like the one from Dr. Weber. This one, rather, was from *American Ninja Warrior* – a call I'd been praying I would get for months now.

Up until then, it was just an ordinary Monday. I had treated patients all day, gotten in a workout, laughed a lot with coworkers, and ate a big salad with turkey for lunch. Just when I was finishing up treating my patients for the evening though, this very excited, youthful-sounding representative from *ANW* called to give me the great news.

"Arianne, I wanted to let you know that you've been accepted to be a competitor on American Ninja Warrior Season 8."

I hurried to inform John after that, my fingers not working nearly fast enough. In fact, I couldn't make them work at all! Or maybe it was my eyes. I literally couldn't find his contact information on my phone.

Then, when I finally had him on the line, I couldn't even get my words out. I was screaming and squealing in excitement so much so that I had to gasp for air.

Next in line, of course, was to call Mom. I was jumping up and down when I called her, too, so she could barely understand me either. Perhaps that was because I was breathing and talking so fast. I couldn't stop smiling though! When I finally did get her to understand what I was saying, she was just as excited.

Then, Dad, of course, gave an enthusiastic, "Great job, Oopie. I'm so proud of you." And then Darren. Between the four of them, complete with their genuine support and happiness, they helped keep me on cloud 9 for quite a while.

Of course, that did mean there were only two weeks until go time. There was so much planning: what to wear, who to invite, T-shirts to get for my friends and family. It was like a whirlwind.

I started with getting "Challenge Accepted" T-shirts. So many of my friends and family purchased them that I was able to donate over $3,000 to the sarcoma fund at Penn Medicine thanks to all their support. Before that point, I hadn't realized exactly how many people were following my story and rallying behind me. It was such an incredible feeling, not to mention very motivating.

Then the night finally came. The moment, too, where I was actually standing at the starting line of the country's toughest obstacle course. It was one of the most exhilarating, intense, and greatest experiences of my life.

There was the warped wall on the far side of numerous obstacles. My ultimate destination was the top of it: the finish line. If you've never seen it on TV – or even if you have – try to picture yourself standing in front of a small house that you need to climb the side of; except that it's slippery and there's someone telling you that you need to touch something on the roof in order to survive.

I knew I had to confront a few other daunting challenges before me to even have a prayer of making that attempt. Although when I looked at each one of them, I remembered the challenges I'd already conquered.

Either I would make it through this particular course or I wouldn't. One way or the other though, I would never forget the experience. That much I knew. I would always let it remind me of how far I'd come and how much more I could achieve.

The lights were so bright as I stood there, waiting for my cue. The timer was huge. The crowd was a blur, and the texture of the mat beneath my sneakers felt soft.

It was difficult to fathom that it was 2:30 in the morning, yet I was so fully awake. I was physically exhausted, but my mind wasn't.

Or was I really awake? Perhaps I was actually dreaming all of this?

I couldn't possibly be really standing there with all those *American Ninja Warrior* Season 8 TV stars. Could I?

It did look totally different in person than on-screen. So much different, beginning with the quin steps – those slanted landing pads that only allowed you a short rest before you had to push off again and bound to the next to keep from sliding off. They were laid out right in front of me.

They looked awfully more difficult, for one thing. Although less intimidating, the water beneath them didn't look so deep.

And the lights… Wow! They were so bright.

The quin steps remind me of a game my friends and I used to play as kids, jumping from one piece of furniture to the next, pretending we would fall into quicksand or a bottomless pit if we missed. That pretended pressure we had in our imaginary world was intense at the time. Now? It was definitely magnified, even though I knew I wouldn't "die" if I missed one. I would only fall up to 10 feet into the cool blue water, which did have a bottom.

Then again, there were no second chances allowed. I had one shot and one shot only.

The quin steps were something I was possibly the most nervous about, primarily because of my leg. I still had quite a bit of swelling in it since a seroma – a pocket of fluid the size of my tumor – had filled in after the mass was removed.

I didn't want to hurt my leg. I wanted it to be strong and powerful enough to get through this first obstacle. Then again, I still had my chemo port on the right side of my chest. So, what's a little swelling?

Three.

Two.

One.

Beeeeep.

The buzzer blared out and the timer began, and I was off. Taking each leap with a great deal of concentration, I took my time and made it to the last step. Of course, in Season 8, they just had to add a rope swing at the end of the quin steps to officially make it to the platform and reach obstacle two.

Technically, it was another obstacle, although they didn't count it that way.

Swinging back and forth a few times, I did have a moment of panic thinking I was going to be stuck there. But after one final swing, I did it after all.

Although the producers had already encouraged us to cheer, smile, and get the crowd riled up, I forgot that part completely. For someone who smiles most of her life, I must have left that at home somehow. It was serious business for me that night.

I also could have paused and caught my breath, but I didn't. I was right on to the second obstacle, the log drop, which is a slick, tree trunk-like central cylindrical beam. You're supposed to wrap your arms and legs around it, and then hang on for dear life as it goes spiraling down a short, but plenty-long-enough path.

Once again, you get just one shot. If you lose your grip, that's it.

I had a great plan for this one. I had noticed earlier back before my name was called that my fellow female competitors all had on short shorts for better skin contact. So, I was planning to pull my pant legs and shirt up. Then, I was going to find my proper grip, one of two options, high or low hand-holds.

That was the plan. However, my intensity got the best of me and I forgot to put any of it into action.

Instead, I grabbed the log, wrapped my legs tightly around it, and went for it. It's all a bit of a blur, but I do remember that first jolt as I held on as tightly as I could. All of that grip training paid off for the first second or two. My hands stayed on, but my legs? Those began to slip all too quickly. By the time the next jolt came, I couldn't sustain my latch any longer.

I fell very gracefully into the "bottomless pit" that was the pool right below.

If I hadn't fallen on that second (or third, depending on if you count the rope) challenge, I would have been on to the next round. It involved hanging from cannon-balls no larger than softballs and swinging over a wall to jump down to the trampoline… which would then set me up for a rolling thunder wheel. That's a large wagon wheel-like object you have to hold onto as it flies overhead.

At least, in my season, that's how it went. Over time, many of the obstacles change and evolve. It's only their main purpose of posing an intense challenge that never falters.

As I walked out of the water, the producers came up to me with a microphone and camera. "Arianne, tell us what happened out there."

I don't even remember being wet at that moment. I do remember responding with, "I don't really know" before they let me walk off.

That wasn't quite right. Because I did know.

I knew I had already conquered the biggest obstacle of my life yet again. So, no matter what happened that night, it was a win.

Although I stepped in the water that night, I rose up higher for it - just by showing up and giving it my all.

21

The Aftermath

*L*ife seemed to get back to normal for a little while after that, though I did continue to train for *ANW*. I was planning to try out again, refusing to let that log drop beat me. I was going to come back even stronger, I told myself. That wasn't such a crazy thought considering how I could train as hard as I wanted now without worrying about radiation, surgery, and chemo.

Not so fast though, it turned out.

Each day seemed like I was getting weaker and weaker, for some reason. I remember trying to do all the normal obstacles that I always did. Yet they took so much more out of me, leaving me wracked with questions that led nowhere good.

Why am I so tired?

Why do I look so pale?

Why am I losing strength this way?

I look like I'm six months pregnant. Do I have some kind of mass? Is the cancer back?

Three people I had inpatient chemotherapy with had passed away during the span of my treatments. I'll never forget Mike, in particular. He was my buddy, a tall and handsome middle-aged man I would walk the halls with often enough. He was always so positive.

Mike had retroperitoneal sarcoma in his abdomen. He had already had it removed before, refusing chemo in the past. I knew him saying yes to it was his last-ditch effort.

Sadly, he passed away shortly after we finished treatment. I went to his funeral service with my mom to support his lovely wife and daughter. It was so tragic how much he'd wanted to live.

That couldn't be what I was dealing with now. It couldn't be that. *Right?*

I thought maybe some foods were making me ill, so I kept eliminating one after another, thinking it would help. It didn't.

The fatigue was getting worse and worse, and my bowel movements were, too. I'd have excruciating pain in my abdomen at times, leaving me even weaker than I already was.

My three-month scans rolled around, leaving me with some definite "scanxiety." I had mentioned to them some of my symptoms, however everything seemed to be okay from an imaging standpoint so they weren't too concerned. Except for this one time. It was the first time I had an abnormal CT scan of my abdomen, which had the doctors telling me I'd have to get an MRI next.

There was nothing to worry about, they told me. It was just to be on the safe side.

After so much experience with cancer, it was just about impossible to not worry though. That was such a big scare, and waiting to hear back was utterly miserable.

The waiting game finally ended, and the results of the MRI came in, indicating that I had a fatty liver.

That made absolutely no sense to me at first. And there were no answers the doctors could give either, leaving me and my loved ones to try to sort it out on our own.

I'm not sure exactly when, but I did start wondering if this newest problem was the result of trying to treat my last one. After all, I was subjected to the most aggressive chemotherapy out there, 10 rounds of antibiotics, blood transfusions, Lupron, and Diflucan; and that was just the start.

I think it's fairly safe to say that my body didn't handle it very well, reacting in ways that weren't "usual" or common more times than I'd like to recall. For example, I remember telling my oncologist that I bled every time I urinated after chemotherapy.

His response was, "That's never happened before."

Mine in return was, "Well, it's happening. Every time."

After that, I got an additional diagnosis of interstitial cystitis. So, I went on to have several additional procedures and appointments.

Then, for about a week before my fifth round of chemotherapy, I was having serious chest pain. It felt like the left side of my heart was beating through my chest with stabbing, searing pain.

Mom and I went in to sit down with my oncologist after that, where I described how it almost felt like I was having a heart attack.

His response was, "Well, it can't be cardiac."

Mine in return was, "Well, it seems like it to me. I need you to order a test to take a look at what's happening."

With much resistance, he ordered an echocardiogram.

The thing is, I am so incredibly tuned in to my body that I know when something is wrong. Just like I found my own tumor, I knew what I was feeling this time shouldn't be shrugged off.

Mom and I left that appointment a little frazzled, a little frustrated, and a little relieved all at the same time. Ultimately, it was worth it when the echocardiogram showed there was a clot in my heart; a three-centimeter clot, possibly from my port.

That's not healthy, to say the least. Therefore, another procedure was scheduled to take care of it.

Now, after all of that was supposed to be a thing of the past, I was dealing with another bewildering but definite unknown. Almost a year went by of me trying to figure things out. I ate so healthy, exercised so regularly, and cut down on as many stressors as I could. Yet, I still felt awful.

Some days, although I never let anyone know, I felt just as bad as when I was in chemo – even worse on occasion. I could barely get through a workday, let alone a workout without feeling like I wanted to crawl in a corner and take a nap.

I was pretty good at powering through. At that point, I knew I could power through anything. So I did, though I didn't give up trying to figure out what was going on.

After looking for months and months for the right person, I found a functional medicine doctor. Functional medicine is a patient-centered approach to try to reach the root of the problem, whatever it might be. When I went for my first appointment, I was a bit overwhelmed, to say the least. There were so many things wrong with me at that point, and talking it all out seemed awful. Even so, it was a necessary first step to a real diagnosis.

It took several appointments and thousands of dollars, but we finally figured out that my body was falling apart.

Small intestinal bacterial overgrowth.

Leaky gut.

Malabsorption of just about all my key nutrients.

Mercury toxicity.

High inflammatory markers.

All of it. My gut had been all but destroyed during treatment. Your gut is 70% of your immune system. All I could think of was that if I am going to prevent cancer from coming back, I'd better heal my gut as soon as possible.

No one ever talks about what happens after treatment. If you look okay, which I did, then everyone thinks that you are okay. Some people would even say I looked great.

I wasn't. Not even a little bit.

It wasn't about to get any better any time soon even with my official diagnosis. Honestly, the journey of healing seemed impossible at the time. First, I tried an elimination diet for 12 weeks with no improvement. If anything, I felt worse.

Then, I switched to a low-FODMAP (Fermentable oligo-, di-, mono-saccharides, and polyols) plan, which seemed to reduce the excruciating abdominal pains I was having. At least I no longer looked like I was pregnant. However, it still didn't solve anything in the end.

After that, they recommended B12 injections for weeks at a time. No improvement there. I did infusions, too, set up the same way I was in chemo, only to feel worse afterward.

Nothing seemed to be helping. My diet was so restrictive, it seemed like disordered eating. Which, considering my past, ended up having emotional effects on me, too.

Beginning to think that I'd never be normal again, I started to get into functional medicine myself and pursued the Institute of Functional Medicine's certification path. As I began to explore treatments and various supplements, there did seem to be a light at the end of the tunnel. Although far off, probably years away, that glimmer was better than nothing – for a little while, anyway.

Yet just when I thought things were slightly improved, I began getting my menstrual cycle every 12 to 14 days, with extremely heavy, heavy bleeding. This went on for over a year, leading to an anemia diagnosis. Because that's the way it goes. If you don't fix the gut issues, it will ultimately lead to hormonal issues as well.

So there I was, exhausted and feeling terrible once again.

Again, no one ever talks about what happens *after* cancer. I think we need to start. Everyone expects your life to go back to the way things were. Back to normal. But that's not always possible. Sometimes it's the very opposite of possible.

People are changed after cancer – emotionally, mentally, physically, and even perhaps spiritually. Movement was what helped me heal emotionally, and it's helped me in so many other ways, too. Yet there is always something hanging over your head after cancer comes to call.

With that said, I will never let that control me. I will never give up on regaining my health. I cherish every day on this Earth and will continue to fight the battle until I'm healthy again. While I'm at it, I will become the best functional medicine provider possible to help others navigate this challenging path.

I might not have wanted this challenge, but it's here and so I'll take it head-on.

22

Dad's Decline

My dad's health was beginning to decline quickly as all of this went on. He was now confined to a wheelchair because his legs were so weak and his ankles were in contracture. Unfortunately, that was only the beginning of his physical problems.

His skin was more and more jaundiced, and even the whites of his eyes weren't white anymore. He couldn't really communicate much anymore, and he was going to the hospital every two weeks for a paracentesis, a procedure where they insert a needle into the abdomen to drain stomach fluid as a result of the cirrhosis. He would get liters taken out each time. Literal liters.

Although Dad was doing so poorly, he opted to have neck surgery to see if it could help with his leg function. Although I knew for sure that wasn't the solution, he was convinced that would help.

It didn't, leading him to have an extended stay in the hospital because he was too weak and confused to go home afterward. Fortunately, his girlfriend of 25 years and recent fiancé, Betsey, did everything she could to take care of him.

I'm so grateful for that because, after so many years of trying to understand addiction, I was sometimes hardened to it. After trying to help, asking him to get help, and encouraging him to stop drinking for so many years, I could never understand why he wouldn't get help.

Was it that he didn't love me the way I thought he did?

Why wouldn't he do it for my brother? Dave hated when he drank.

Didn't he want to be around for me?

All of that may sound irrational. Though, it was how I felt so many times over and over again.

Ultimately, I know my dad loved me; it was himself he didn't love. He was a star quarterback in high school, going on to play at Oklahoma State, a D1 university. Then, he hurt his knee there and had to leave the game he loved. He was deployed to Vietnam as a medical technician shortly thereafter.

To this day, I can't even begin to imagine what he saw or experienced there. Although judging from the stories I heard and letters I read, I believe he was never the same after that. Add to that his son getting cancer, and it was all too much for him.

I think that was the hardest part for me: the difference between him and David. It's the one thing I could never really understand: how hard my brother fought for his life and how my dad was throwing his away.

After the neck surgery, he was in and out of rehabilitation hospitals and then admitted to the Veterans Affairs hospital on multiple occasions. I don't think he ever really realized why he felt so bad: why the choices he'd made over the course of his life led him to have end-stage cirrhosis.

The last time he was in the hospital was horrifying. He was completely out of his mind, and his body was in fast decline. I tried to sit with him and calm him down, but there was nothing I could do. Come to find out, he couldn't process the medications they were giving him.

I was so heartbroken when I left that day, thinking I had just said goodbye to him forever.

Rather, it wasn't until months later that he passed away, and it was at his home while I was lying next to him. I wish I could say it was peaceful, but it wasn't.

So many thoughts were racing through my mind, like how I watched my brother suffer so much at the end, too. It was all so heart-wrenching.

There were countless memories that kept surfacing in the following days. Like the time I went to Dad's house and he could barely talk or stand up. I was so upset but didn't know what to do for him other than to take him to the emergency room. I had no idea what they would do for him there, but I knew there was no way I could help.

Then there were other memories, like how we went to New York together – just the two of us – and walked the Brooklyn Bridge. And when he walked me down the aisle – a day I will never forget.

He *loved me*.
I *know he loved me*.
I *just wish he would have stopped drinking*.

I would always remind myself that he had an addiction – that he had a disease. But I have to confess: I just never understood it.

As much as I know about addiction from a logical perspective, I don't know if I'll ever really get it emotionally. All I can do is make him proud, just like I promised my brother.

23

Rise Up

Following my difficult cancer journey, the challenging and exciting American Ninja Warrior competition, and my TEDx speaking event, my purpose and vision began to crystallize. When I stood on the TEDx stage with the light shining on me and shared my story of healing through mindset, nutrition, and movement to hundreds of attendees, I realized how many of us share similar stories. How many of us face challenges of our own. How many of us have the power to rise up.

As with most of life's experiences, we gain from what we give. Working through everything that has happened in my life, both the challenges and opportunities, and sharing my story publicly has been powerfully healing.

We are all faced with challenges in life. Take a moment to think about a challenge or obstacle that you have had to overcome. Some can be overwhelming and life-changing like divorce, death, and disease, and some less impactful like public speaking or making a career change. To each of you, that challenge was significant and that is what is most important.

My brother is my hero. I observed and admired his courage and unrelenting tenacity during his battle. I learned many important and beautiful lessons from him and made an unwavering commitment to him and his memory. First, I told him that I would live my life in honor of him and always make him proud. Second, I began living with passion and purpose. Third, I realized life is a true gift to treasure.

My mother's sole purpose was to provide love and support to my brother and me during our fights against cancer. Grace is defined as how you accept winning and losing, good and bad luck, and darkness and light. My beautiful mother is the true definition of grace. I am so blessed to have her as my best friend, confidant, and travel-the-world partner.

My Dad is watching over me and I know that he gave me my free spirit, love of travel, and passion for life. I hope he is looking down saying, "I'm proud of you, Oopie."

Although everyone tells John regularly how lucky he is to be with me, we both know the truth. I am, in fact, the luckiest woman in the world to be supported and loved by a truly honorable and devoted man.

Each challenge that I faced has brought a tremendous opportunity. Starting with becoming the sole owner of CORE Fitness at age 22 shortly after my brother's passing, and then pursuing my doctorate of physical therapy while maintaining my business. Then working full-time as a therapist and director at a reputable PT practice. Each challenge and achievement has led me to exactly where I am right now – where I should be.

When I gained clarity on my mission and vision, the doors to the Movement Paradigm Integrative Health Center opened. It's a place where we help people heal their bodies, alleviate inflammation, interact with the world better, and live with vitality through mindset reframing, nutrition, and movement. We use a functional medicine, patient-centered, whole-person approach to identify and address the underlying causes of health issues, rather than simply treating the symptoms.

Each day I am blessed to have the opportunity to help individuals become the best versions of themselves. As one of my cherished clients said, "Arianne has made my life better in so many ways! I came to her overweight and with a knee that was extremely painful and had limited mobility. I've always been athletic, but before Arianne, I wasn't able to do the activities I love. With her guidance and vast knowledge in so many different areas (mindset, nutrition, movement), I've lost over 60 pounds and gained so much strength that I am now doing pull-ups and handstands! And I also no longer need cholesterol medicine!"

That is exactly the approach to health that people deserve.

This is my goal in life – both for myself and for you. I have overcome some of my biggest challenges through mindset, nutrition, and movement. This is my story, one I hope will inspire you to rise up stronger, to take ownership of your health by tapping into your personal power.

No one is promised tomorrow. What some people take for granted, others are fighting for. So, let's do everything we can to appreciate what we have in the moment and what we can achieve if we only try.

Movement has helped me heal my pain, express my emotions, and give me not only physical strength, but emotional, mental, and spiritual strength, too. Movement makes me feel alive, bringing music to my soul. It is poetry in motion: a gift that should never be taken for granted.

Each day is a gift. Treasure it. Treasure yourself. Eat to nourish your body, move well and often, and fill your mind with hope, happiness, and gratitude.

Let's rise up together. When we do, we never know what truly amazing things can happen.

About the Author

Dr. Arianne Missimer is an award-winning Doctor of Physical Therapy, Registered Dietitian, Registered Yoga Teacher, and Mindfulness Educator. She is the Founder of the Movement Paradigm, an integrative health center focusing on mindset, nutrition, and movement; blending Eastern and Western philosophies, rooted in neuroscience, functional medicine, and movement science. (themovementparadigm.com).

She continues to strive for excellence and has received numerous awards for her contributions to the health field including the National Strength and Conditioning Association Sports Medicine Rehabilitation Specialist of the Year, American Dietetic Association Recognized Young Dietitian of the Year, University of Delaware Outstanding Alumni, Neumann University Physical Therapy Alumni, *Mainline Today* Health Care Hero, and *Mainline Today* Power Women.

Dr. Missimer is a TEDx and keynote speaker, where she has addressed universities, conferences, Chambers of Commerce, colleges, summits, and more. She also presents nationally and internationally in the areas of movement science, nutrition, and mindfulness.

As a cancer survivor, mover, athlete, and American Ninja Warrior competitor herself, she is dedicated to educating professionals and the community and helping you lead your best life through powerful dietary interventions, movement, sleep, and mindset reframing techniques; to empower you to heal your body, alleviate inflammation, and live with vitality.

Acknowledgments

Immeasurable appreciation and deepest gratitude for their help and support are extended to the following persons, who have contributed to making this possible:

For Dave
You have given me passion and purpose. Your courageous spirit lives in my heart, always.

For Mom
You have provided me with endless love, encouragement, and support during all of life's ups and downs. I am forever grateful to have you as a mentor, friend, and hero.

For Dad
Thank you for always believing in me. I know you are looking over me and I promise to make you proud.

For John
Thank you for always supporting me and my dreams. My heart, my soul, and my life are full because of you.

For Dr. Darren Rodia
You have supported me during my journey and inspired me to make this a reality.

For Kim Dare

I am forever grateful for your mentorship, friendship, and direction in leading me where I am today.

For Jeannette DiLouie

Your knowledge, guidance, and suggestions have been invaluable.

For Lois Hoffman

Thank you for the guidance and assistance in bringing my story to life.

For Dave Kinzeler

Thank you for your talent, expertise, and patience in making the artwork beautiful.

For JoAnna Schneck

Your contributions to polishing the book have been invaluable and I am forever grateful for what you have brought to my life.

Stay Connected!

Make sure to follow us on social media for daily tips to help you heal your body, move well, alleviate inflammation, and live with vitality.

Facebook: @TheMovementParadigm

Instagram: @themovementparadigm

YouTube: @TheMovementParadigm

Twitter: @theMvmtParadigm

TikTok: @themovementparadigm

LinkedIn: @DrArianneMissimer

For media appearances, interviews, and speaking inquiries, visit www.drariannemissimer.com.

If you want to feel empowered to take ownership of your health and be the best version of yourself, sign up for our weekly newsletter.

Websites: www.themovementparadigm.com and www.drariannemissimer.com

If you enjoyed this book, please make sure to leave a review!

Printed in Great Britain
by Amazon

83548156R00142